NOLO
Products & Services

"In Nolo you can trust." —THE NEW YORK TIMES

Books & Software

Nolo publishes hundreds of great books and software programs on the topics consumers and business owners want to know about. And every one of them is available in print or as a download at Nolo.com.

Plain-English Legal Dictionary

Free at Nolo.com. Stumped by jargon? Look it up in America's most up-to-date source for definitions of cutting edge legal terminology. Emphatically not your grandmother's law dictionary!

Legal Encyclopedia

Free at Nolo.com. Here are more than 1,200 free articles and answers to frequently asked questions about everyday consumer legal issues including wills, bankruptcy, small business formation, divorce, patents, employment and much more. As *The Washington Post* says, "Nobody does a better job than Nolo."

Online Legal Forms

Make a will, or living trust, form an LLC or corporation or obtain a trademark or provisional patent at Nolo.com, all for a remarkably affordable price. In addition, our site provides hundreds of high-quality, low-cost downloadable legal forms including bills of sale, promissory notes, nondisclosure agreements and many more.

Lawyer Directory

Find an attorney at Nolo.com. Nolo's unique lawyer directory provides in-depth profiles of lawyers all over America. From fees and experience to legal philosophy, education and special expertise, you'll find all the information you need to pick a lawyer who's a good fit.

Nolo's Aim:
to make the law...

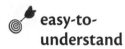 **easy-to-understand**

 **affordable**

 **hassle free**

Keep Up to Date!

Old law is often bad law. That's why Nolo.com has free updates for this and every Nolo book. And if you want to be notified when a revised edition of any Nolo title comes out, sign up for this free service at nolo.com/legalupdater.

"Nolo is always there in a jam."
—NEWSWEEK

First edition

Selling Your House in a Tough Market

10 Strategies That Work

by Ilona Bray & Alayna Schroeder

NOLO

FIRST EDITION	MAY 2009
Editor	MARCIA STEWART
Cover Design	JALEH DOANE
Book Design	SUSAN PUTNEY
Proofreading	SUSAN CARLSON GREENE
Index	ELLEN SHERRON
Printing	DELTA PRINTING SOLUTIONS, INC.

Bray, Ilona M., 1962-

Selling your house in a tough market : 10 strategies that work / by Ilona Bray and Alayna Schroeder. -- 1st ed.

p. cm.

Includes index.

ISBN-13: 978-1-4133-1035-1 (pbk.)

ISBN-10: 1-4133-1035-4 (pbk.)

1. House selling--United States. 2. Residential real estate--United States. I. Schroeder, Alayna, 1975- II. Title.

HD259.B73 2009

643'.120973--dc22

2009009115

Quantity sales: For information on bulk purchases or corporate premium sales, please contact the Special Sales Department. For academic sales or textbook adoptions, ask for Academic Sales. Call 800-955-4775 or write to Nolo, 950 Parker Street, Berkeley, CA 94710.

Acknowledgments

Great books about complex, detailed, and ever-changing topics are rarely written alone. We were fortunate not to have to even *try* to cover all the topics in this book without the help of many knowledgeable, experienced professionals.

First off, we couldn't have done it without the excellent advice and counsel of our advisory board. All of them devoted their time and expertise to discussing current market issues, sharing their insights, and reviewing selected chapters of this book. This intrepid crew includes:

- **Asheesh Advani,** founder of Virgin Money, USA, based in Waltham, Massachusetts (www.virginmoneyus.com), and an expert in alternative forms of home financing

- **Nancy Atwood,** Designated Broker with ZipRealty in Framingham, Massachusetts (www.ziprealty.com)

- **George Devine,** licensed real estate broker in San Francisco and author and educator in the real estate field

- **Stephen Fishman,** a Bay Area attorney, tax expert, and author (many of his books are available at www.nolo.com)

- **Jaan Henry,** broker/owner of Jaan Henry & Co., Realtors® in Montclair, New Jersey and the owner of a relocation network of real estate agents across the United States

- **Kym Hough,** owner of Staged to Sell in Danville, California (www.staged-to-sell.com), and www.StagersList.com, an online resource for stagers

- **Joel G. Kinney,** partner with Goldstein & Herndon, LLP, in Chestnut Hill, Massachusetts

- **Mark Nash,** Associate Broker with Coldwell Banker, who serves the Chicago, Evanston, Skokie, and Wilmette areas of Illinois (www.mark nashrealtor.com), and author of *1001 Tips for Buying & Selling a Home*

- **Janet Portman,** attorney, author, Nolo editor, and syndicated columnist, and

- **Paul A. Rude,** professional inspector and owner of Summer Street Inspections, based in Berkeley, California (www.summerinspect.com).

In addition to these knowledgeable professionals, we also received important input from Karen Cabot, owner of Clutter Cutter (www.cluttercutter.net) in Pasadena, California; Kimberly Dragone, Executive Mortgage Banker at William Raveis Mortgage in Newton Centre, Massachusetts; Steve Elias, author of *The Foreclosure Survival Guide* (Nolo); Richard Leshnower, a New York-based attorney with specialized experience in real estate; and Rick Woods, Realtor® in Tampa Bay, Florida. We also appreciated the stories of homebuyers and sellers, including Josh and Gillian Viers and Skip and Adele Ohs.

Of course, we're also grateful to our wonderful colleagues at Nolo. Special thanks to Marcia Stewart, Nolo's acquisitions editor, who made sure this book became a possibility. The book also had the support and input from Nolo's CEO Jake Warner and VP of Editorial Mary Randolph. A big thanks to Jaleh Doane, Emma Cofod, and Susan Putney in our Production department for making the book look so good.

Table of Contents

Your Home-Selling Companion

The real estate market has been on quite the roller coaster ride lately, leaving few parts of the United States unaffected. And as a homeowner, the stress is unavoidable—you have little choice but to watch to see whether your investment gains or loses in the coming months or years.

Of course, your stress levels may start ticking upward even faster if you want—or perhaps urgently need—to sell your house. Will you find a willing buyer, or will your house sit unnoticed, with "For Sale" and "Price Reduction" signs out front? Is there any hope of turning a profit, or will you be lucky to sell for enough to cover your mortgage? If the sale doesn't work out sometime soon, are you at risk of losing your house to foreclosure?

Fortunately, there's no need to be paralyzed by uncertainty. This book—which features advice and insights from a nationwide team of real estate experts—will help you understand the current market realities and how to successfully navigate them. You'll learn how to avoid the mistakes made by other home sellers and how to go the extra mile to really make your house stand out and attract prospective buyers.

With the right information and planning, you'll be able to position your house for a quick and smooth sale. The book will guide you through ten useful selling strategies, showing you how to:

- set the right price from the beginning, a crucial step for attracting buyer interest

- investigate and deal with your house's repair needs so buyers won't either be turned off or be able to negotiate you into a corner

- "stage" your house inside and out, so that it looks too good to pass up

- find the best real estate agent to advise you about local market conditions, carry out an effective marketing strategy, and help you finalize the sale

- market and sell your house without the help of a real estate agent, if you're motivated to save on commission payments
- offer special incentives to bring in buyers and their agents
- advertise and market the house creatively
- know when and how to shift strategy if the house isn't selling
- earn rental money if you decide to take the house off the market for an extended time, and finally
- negotiate with a buyer, create a mutually agreeable contract, and close the sale.

Of course, much of the heavy lifting will be done by your real estate agent, assuming you hire one. But selling a house is a team effort, and you'll be best able to weigh strategies with your agent and make intelligent decisions when negotiating with buyers if you've learned a thing or two first. Here at Nolo, we have a long history of putting tough concepts into plain English to make the learning process easy. We hope you'll use this book as a handy guide along the way to successfully selling your home. ●

Know Your Market and Price It Right

Meet Your Adviser

Nancy Atwood, with ZipRealty (www.ZipRealty.com), based in Framingham, Massachusetts; Nancy is a Designated Broker, responsible for the legal compliance and mentoring of real estate agents who directly serve buyers and sellers

What she does:	Nancy started with ZipRealty as an agent, where she helped countless home buyers and sellers. She moved up to her current position as a broker and is now responsible for 190 full-service buyer and seller agents statewide. She was named a ZipRealty outstanding employee of the year in 2006. Atwood's pre-real estate experience includes 25 years in the high-tech industry doing customer service, sales, and marketing.
Favorite money-saving strategy in tough times:	"Take a deep breath and ask yourself, will I regret NOT purchasing this item five years from now, or can I live without it?"
Likes best about her work:	"Listening and finding solutions."
Strangest thing she's seen sellers do:	"I had some sellers who decided to paint their house yellow and purple because it was springtime and they thought being different would help them sell their home quicker. They surprised me with this. It didn't help!"
Top tip for sellers:	"People like to imagine themselves living in the home they are considering purchasing. Remove family photos and personal items, so that they can dream."

I f you're like most homeowners, when it comes time to sell, getting the best possible price is your number one motivator. You're hoping to make a profit—or at least minimize your loss—before moving on. But on the other side of the table sits a buyer who has the opposite objective: to pay as little as possible. That makes your job a tricky one. You'll have to set a price you're willing to accept that's attractive enough to capture the interest of potential buyers. Make a mistake and you may find no one will even look at your property or that, with the weeks and months ticking by, you have to drop the price by many thousands of dollars to get any offers. Or (less commonly, especially in a cold market), price too low and you'll find that you're walking away from the transaction with less than you really should have.

So how do you find that perfect balance between underpricing and overpricing? Your real estate agent, if you hire one, should help you with this, but it's also important to educate yourself. You need to know what to expect when you offer your house for sale, so you'll be ready to negotiate from the best possible position, convincing buyers that your property is a good deal at a reasonable price. This chapter will help you do that, by covering how to:

- gauge your local real estate market
- set a realistic price
- make sure you can afford to sell, and
- consider alternatives if selling is impossible or undesirable.

Is the Market Hot or Cold?

Whether a house will be easy or difficult to sell depends on more than just the desirability of the house itself—it also depends heavily on the "temperature" of the market.

As a seller, you'd be happiest with a "hot" market, in which there are more buyers than sellers. Well-priced houses in hot markets usually sell quickly, as buyers compete to get their foot in the door, sometimes even paying more than the asking price. Only the true duds or grossly overpriced houses get rejected by this anxious flock of househunters, so the overall inventory of available homes stays low. Sellers often receive multiple offers and can confidently negotiate deals, knowing that if they don't get what they want, another offer will come along soon. The seller may even benefit from waiting, as prices in hot markets tend to climb.

Unfortunately, when this book went to print, real estate markets in most of the United States were cold—freezing cold. In a cold market, there are more sellers than buyers and a high inventory of available houses, which often languish on the market for some time. Buyers can typically make less than full-price offers and negotiate for other concessions, knowing that the seller might not get another offer anytime soon—or at least not before the costs of maintaining the house force the seller to drop its price. Pricing is more competitive, and sellers may have to offer creative incentives to try to catch the attention of the relatively few buyers.

> **TIP**
>
> **Markets can be balanced, too.** Rather than strictly hot or cold, in balanced markets, there are about an equal number of sellers and buyers. Prices don't tend to be either rock bottom or sky high. A balanced market is usually transitional, though—at some point, it's going to tip toward hot (as more buyers realize it's a good time to buy because prices are reasonable) or cold (when lots of sellers become motivated to put their homes on the market, because there seem to be plenty of interested buyers).

Though you may be reading doom-and-gloom media accounts of the U.S. real estate market, don't leave it at that: Take a closer look at what's happening your local area. Even when U.S. real estate is at a lowest point, there will still be localized hot markets. Here are some of the objective indicators that will help you figure out what's going on locally:

- **Average sales price.** Looking at recent sales can give you a good idea of how much homes are actually selling for. You're looking in particular for prices of comparable homes, or "comps" in real estate lingo. That means homes of a similar size and quality, sold recently (within six months or less) in the same locale (ideally within six blocks in an urban area, but stopping at any dividing lines like a large street that changes the neighborhood character). You can research sale prices yourself, but a real estate professional should also provide this information, if you're working with one. If the average sales price is falling, that's an indicator of a cold market.

- **Days on market.** Another important piece of information is the average number of days it takes houses in your area to sell. The longer homes remain unsold, the more likely that market is cold. This number is very predictive, too—when it starts climbing, it's an early indicator that the market is cooling.

Upward Trend

In 2008, the median sales price of existing homes in the United States was $198,000. In 1970, it was $65,300.

- **Inventory.** The "inventory" is the number of houses on the market compared to the average number of buyers in that market. For example, if 4,000 houses are currently for sale and 1,000 houses sell (on average) each month, there's four months' worth of inventory. The more inventory, the cooler the market is likely to be.

According to Forbes magazine, here are 25 markets predicted to be strong in 2009:

McAllen, Texas	Austin, Texas	Birmingham, Alabama
Syracuse, New York	Rochester, New York	Forth Worth, Texas
Pittsburgh, Pennsylvania	San Antonio, Texas	New Orleans, Louisiana
Buffalo, New York	Augusta, Georgia	Dallas, Texas
El Paso, Texas	Baton Rouge, Louisiana	Indianapolis, Indiana
Tulsa, Oklahoma	Memphis, Tennessee	Columbia, South Carolina
Houston, Texas	Oklahoma City, Oklahoma	Scranton, Pennsylvania
Charleston, South Carolina	Albany, New York	Omaha, Nebraska
Little Rock, Arkansas		

RESOURCE

Get market information yourself. You can find a lot of helpful information, including average sale prices and days on the market, on websites such as www.trulia.com, www.domania.com, and www.zillow.com, for little or no cost. Also check the website of your state's Realtor® association.

Every House Is Different

As we've mentioned, even the coldest markets contain pockets of heat. In fact, your particular house may be hot, perhaps because it's one of the best-looking places in a popular neighborhood. Without being overoptimistic, you'll want to recognize when your house is hot. And if your house is cold or market balanced, you'll want to do everything you can to heat it up.

Begin by evaluating your neighborhood. Pay particular attention to the factors discussed in the last section: Are your neighborhood statistics better, worse, or about the same as the rest of the surrounding area? For example, if homes in your neighborhood are selling quickly and for their full asking prices, your neighborhood may be hot, even if the general market in the area isn't.

Usually, a particular neighborhood is hot for some identifiable reason. It might be located near an attractive feature, like a beach, or have the best schools in the region. It may be an older, established neighborhood of historic homes in a sea of new developments. If you know your neighborhood has a feature that makes it more desirable than those surrounding it, factor that in when evaluating the market's temperature. Look only at comps in your desirable neighborhood, not the next one over—even if it's only a couple of blocks away.

Now, back to your own house. Does it have exceptional characteristics that will attract buyers? You may find, for example, that large, expensive homes in your neighborhood are selling slowly, because few buyers can afford them. However, if you have a smaller home in the same neighborhood it may sell quickly as people try to break into the market or get into a good school district.

Make Your House Hot

What's the best way to turn up the heat under your house? The key is to convince potential buyers that your house is a better deal than the rest, either because it has unique and desirable features or because it's offered at a better price. For example, if you have a three-bedroom, two-bath house in a neighborhood where most three bedrooms have only one bath, play up the second bath as an added bonus.

In a down market, the easiest and most typical way to make your house stand out is to have the lowest price among comparable homes. We'll explain more about that in this chapter. But it's not the only way to garner interest and increase visitor traffic. As we'll explain throughout this book, you can do many things to make your house better than the rest, from decorating it perfectly to offering special incentives. For now, just know that the more attractive and intriguing you can make the total package, the more likely you are to sell quickly, no matter how dismal the market.

What matters most?

According to a 2007 report by the National Association of Realtors®, buyers today are particularly drawn to:

- oversized garages
- air conditioning
- a walk-in closet in the master bedroom
- hardwood floors, and
- granite countertops

It Pays to Start With the Right Sales Price

Setting the right price from the start is among the most important steps toward successfully selling your home. As Rick Woods, a Realtor® in Tampa Bay, Florida, puts it, "The real estate mantra used to be location, location, location. Now it's price, price, price."

Most sellers think of their houses as special and better than similar homes. Some may even tour open houses in the neighborhood and smugly tell themselves, "Well, my garden looks a lot better than this one, so we should be able to get more," or "This bathroom may be remodeled, but it doesn't even have a double vanity." Your house no doubt has some great things about it that the others on the market don't.

But don't forget that living in a house can also make you blind to its faults. For many sellers, relying on this inherent sense of superiority is a critical mistake, because they forget to look at the house through the unsentimental eyes of prospective buyers. They then set too high a price, which ironically enough can ultimately result in selling the property for too little. Here's why.

The Right Price Helps Bring in Buyers

When a house is priced too high, especially in a down market, it typically generates little interest. Buyers who have lots of different options may not even look at it, believing the seller is unrealistic about the home's true value. They may assume the seller is out of touch with current market realities and won't accept a reasonable price or that the seller will be particularly tight-fisted or difficult to work with. Even if potential buyers take a look, they'll rarely come for a second showing. In fact, real estate professionals may take clients to an overpriced house purely to convince them that another, cheaper property is a good deal, thus helping them close the latter sale.

On the other hand, when a seller sets the price at or even a little below the home's true market value, buyer interest perks up. Potential purchasers will act quickly, fearing that if they don't take advantage of the good deal, someone else will.

You may think, "Well, I'd rather wait a few months and get what I think this place is worth." But the longer a house sits on the market, the less desirable it becomes. Buyers begin to wonder whether there's something wrong with the place. Those who are mildly interested begin speculating about whether the seller is getting desperate enough to accept a lower price—perhaps much lower. As new competition enters the market, fewer buyers will even bother looking. And, of course, until you sell the place, you'll be handling mortgage, insurance, utility, and maintenance expenses. Particularly if you've already bought a new home, this can get expensive, potentially wiping out any profit you make by holding out for a higher price.

EXAMPLE: Ed and Sharon plan to put their home on the market. There's a comparably sized home down the street listed for $275,000, but it doesn't have the charming porch or leaded glass windows that their house does, and the carpet is an ugly green color, while Ed and Sharon have hardwood floors. Ed and Sharon decide these improvements mean their house should be able to fetch at least $300,000. They move to a new home and list the house for sale.

But Ed and Sharon don't see some other important differences between the homes. The other house has one more bathroom than theirs does, and the kitchen is recently remodeled, while theirs is 15 years old. The other house also has a bigger yard. These factors increase other the property's relative value.

A couple months later, the house down the street has sold, while Ed and Sharon's is still on the market with no offers. Worried, they drop the price to $285,000. Still no interest, and in the meantime, prices are falling. Three months pass, and they drop the price again, to $265,000. By now, their listing is "stale." Buyers notice it has sat unsold for five months, and few even bother to visit. Sensing an opportunity, a buyer finally offers $250,000, and Ed and Sharon agree to the sale—for far less than they might have been able to get five months earlier, and have paid mortgage and maintenance costs in the meantime.

The Right Price Avoids Desperation

Those buyers who try to sniff out desperation are often right—sellers who hold on for too long really can go into a panic. They may start to worry that the place will never sell or feel additional pressure to drop the price and get out quickly, especially if housing prices are declining or if they've already moved on to a new home. Their hope drops to all-time lows as the phone stops ringing and literally no one takes a look at the house, making it all too obvious that no offers are about to arrive.

If you set the right price up front, you'll avoid this feeling of desperation. Not only are you more likely to get one or more good offers, you'll be in a better negotiating position with the offers you receive. If a potential purchaser proposes terms that you don't think are reasonable, you can counteroffer or even reject the offer with some confidence that another one will come along.

In a Down Market, Don't Buy Before You Sell

It's not uncommon, when you're selling one house and buying another, to find the house you want to purchase before you've sold your current home. This is especially true in a down market, when you're likely to come across some pretty good bargains.

In these situations, you usually have to come up with some way to make payments on both mortgages. You have several different options: You can simply pay both out of pocket, if you can afford to; you can take out a home equity loan or line of credit on your current home; or you can borrow from someone you know or another source. There are even special "bridge" loans for this exact situation, but they're expensive.

None of these options are ideal. After all, if it takes longer than you expect to sell your current home, you may have much higher expenses than you can comfortably afford long term. And unless you rent out your old home—unlikely if you're planning on selling it—you won't have any additional income with which to offset the high costs. You might become the classic desperate seller, anxious to get rid of your house at any price.

For this reason, we don't advocate buying a new house in a down market before selling your old one, if you can avoid it. You'll be in the worst possible negotiating position as a seller. And keep in mind—there's more than one bargain to be had as a buyer in a down market. Better to wait for the next one and avoid becoming a desperate seller.

Is the Price Right?

Setting the right price is all well and good in theory, but how do you do it in practice? You've already begun the process by evaluating the heat of the local market and how your house fits within that. Now, you simply need to take a closer look at what other houses are selling for to judge the relative value of your home, called its "fair market value." No matter how priceless you think your remodeled kitchen or in-ground pool are, the market sets a value—the price a buyer is willing to pay. Here are some steps you can take to make sure your price is competitive.

> **CAUTION**
> **Pricing isn't about your own needs.** As broker and adviser George Devine explains, "Some people set their price based on what I call a 'need basis' rather than a 'market basis'—they look at what they think they need to achieve to pay off their current mortgage and afford their next house and go from there. Unfortunately, that has no relation to what buyers will pay."

Get Outside Evidence

To compare your house to others on the market, you'll want to look at:

- **A comparative market analysis.** A "CMA" is a report, often but not necessarily compiled by a real estate professional, that gives you information about houses similar to yours (in size, amenities, and location) that are either on the market, have sold, or were listed but expired (usually, because they were priced too high and no one bought) within a reasonably recent time period (ideally three months when the market is in transition and no more than six months). These sales can tell you what homes like yours are actually selling for, how long it's taking for them to sell, and what their sale prices are in relation to their list prices. It's especially important to pay attention to the prices of pending, rather than closed, sales, for the basic reason that they're the most recent. (And in a falling market, the appropriate price for the house you want to buy may be even less than the most recent pending comps.)

TIP

You can get a CMA without hiring a real estate professional. Some websites, such as www.homegain.com, offer a comparative market analysis for free. These are usually prepared by a local real estate agent who will contact you and probably try to solicit your business. If you don't mind the hard sell, it's a way to get the information even without hiring the agent. Alternatively, you can pay a small fee for such a report, generated online. For example, at ushomevalue.com, $40 will buy you a one-time "appraisal emulation report" that lists several comparable properties that have sold in your neighborhood. That's a step up from what you'll get from online appraisal systems, like those on www.zillow.com, which will estimate your home's worth, but aren't always up to date and won't give you immediate access to the comparative information that underlies their estimates.

- **List prices versus sale prices.** You also want to know the difference between what people are asking for their homes and what they are actually getting. This will prevent you from unrealistically valuing your property, for example by thinking, "That house down the street was on sale for $250,000—I should be able to get at least $315,000!" If the house actually sold for $225,000, you may be better off pricing lower to start with, to generate more immediate interest.

- **A professional appraisal.** When you bought your house, the bank probably required you to get it "appraised"—that is, have a professional view it and put a dollar figure on its market value. Banks do this to protect their own interests, because if you overpay for a property and can't make your mortgage payments, the bank won't be able to sell the property for what you owe on it. But you can pay to get an appraisal too, just to evaluate your house's market value. Usually, the appraiser will give you a report that arrives at the value of your property by comparing it to others that have recently sold. But keep in mind—in most case, the appraiser won't have actually have seen the comparable properties (while a real estate agent might have). An appraisal should cost around $300–$400.

- **Real estate agents.** Even if you don't end up hiring a real estate agent (we'll discuss the option of selling the property yourself in Chapter 5), it's a good idea to get a few of their opinions as to how much your house is worth. An agent will usually offer an opinion if he or she thinks there's any possibility of being hired. The benefits are that agents are familiar with the local market and can base their estimates on actually seeing the house. Chances are they toured through the other local houses that recently sold, too. "Sellers almost always estimate high," says adviser and seasoned real estate broker Nancy Atwood. "An agent who really knows the market has seen what there is to see and can really set the seller straight, making sure they start out with the right price that will attract buyers." Don't use this as your only source of information, though—if agents think there's a chance you'll hire them, they may suggest an artificially high value to convince you you're best off listing with them. This is called "buying" the listing. (As we'll discuss in Chapter 4, the best agents will make their recommendations based on the CMA, which they'll provide to you.)

- **Open houses.** Although it's the least scientific measurement, open houses in your neighborhood, even of the houses that aren't quite comparable to yours, will also be informative. Viewing other houses helps you get a real sense of what drives list prices up and down—and, if you listen to some conversations, how buyers are reacting to the price.

Between the list of comparable properties, the opinions of agents, a possible appraisal report, and your own hard look at your house and others, you'll probably arrive at a likely value—or at least a range, most likely within around $10,000 to $25,000.

TIP

Visit some comparables yourself. If you're working with an agent, ask the agent to show you some comparable properties. "Sometimes sellers are so attached to their homes, they think they're worth more than comparable properties," says adviser Nancy Atwood, broker with ZipRealty. "Looking at comparable properties yourself is a good way to make sure you set a realistic price."

If the opinions you're getting are still all over the map, do some more research. For example, taking a closer look at the comparable properties might reveal that a particularly low-priced one needs a new foundation or a particularly high-priced one is actually located across a school district boundary, in a better district.

Set the Price: High, Low, or in Between?

Now that you have a good sense of what your house is worth, you'll have to decide what to do with the information. You have three options:

- **Set the asking price below the market value.** You stand the best chance of generating a lot of interest if you set a price that's a little below what other similar homes are listed for. Potential buyers will see there's a bargain to be had and, hopefully, come running. Of course, that may mean you end up selling to one of them for a little less than market value.

- **Set the asking price right at the market value.** You may want to put your house on the market for exactly what it's worth. A fair price should generate some buyer interest, but you're likely to get offers below the asking price, especially in a down market. And you won't have much room to negotiate if you're really intent on getting your price.

- **Set the asking price above market value.** If you set your price above the market value, fewer people may come to look at the property. (If no one comes to look at all, that's probably a good indicator that you're way off base pricewise.) Though you may figure this will give you plenty of wiggle room if you receive an offer below your asking price, keep in mind that your pool of potential buyers will probably be smaller, in part because fewer people will look at the place and, in part, because many who do may think you're unrealistic and not bother to make an offer. You could even be helping your competition, by making their homes look reasonably priced by comparison.

TIP

Just a tad above market value can work. A house that seems overpriced by a mere $10,000 won't drive away as many buyers as one that seems $50,000 too high. Buyers are apt to think that you're willing to negotiate and haven't completely lost your mind when it comes to the home's actual value.

So if every price level has its disadvantages, what should you do? Your best bet is to keep your house on the lower end of the range of comparable homes for sale. For example, if there are four comparable homes in the neighborhood listed at $375,000, $350,000, $335,000, and $325,000, you'll grab the most attention by pricing your house somewhere between the middle and lower end—say, at $339,000. Anything above the top price in the range, and your house is likely to be ignored. Then again, if your house really belongs at the top, you'll want to advertise and highlight the features that make it stand out, such as extra square footage or an updated kitchen and bath.

$399,900 Versus $400,000: What's the Big Difference?

If you've ever looked on the Internet for a house—and according to the National Association of Realtors®, 77% of home buyers do—you've probably seen houses at prices hovering just below a seemingly huge number, like $399,900 instead of $400,000. It's not an unfamiliar tactic—after all, 99 cents still sounds cheaper (and is, slightly) than one dollar.

But there's an important reason sellers do this that extends beyond buyer psychology. Many online databases give buyers the option to look at homes in a certain price range: for example, between $375,000 and $399,999 ($25,000 price points are pretty common, both when setting database search criteria and in buyers' minds, when they think about how much they can afford). By pricing your home just below a cutoff amount, you can maximize the number of people looking at it, because buyers are usually willing to look *below* their maximum price points but not above them.

TIP

Keep track of changes in the market even after you've set your price. If the market is softening and new listings are coming in at even lower prices or other sellers are adjusting their asking prices downward, you could soon find yourself at the top of the range, looking like the unrealistic or unreasonable seller. To avoid this, refresh your market research every month that your house remains unsold, then decide whether you're willing to adjust your price. (See Chapter 8 for further discussion on what to do if your house isn't selling.)

Can You Afford to Sell?

Ideally, the value of your home has increased since you purchased it. And unless you took out significant home equity loans, you'll cash out on this entire nest egg when you sell. But, what if your price research suggests that you might have to sell at a loss or will only break even?

You wouldn't be alone. In the last few years, prices in many parts of the United States have dropped significantly. Combined with popular loan products that allowed borrowers to make very low down payments or none at all, some homeowners now owe more on their homes than the properties are worth. Unless they have additional cash to pay off their mortgages when they sell, these would-be sellers can't afford to get out.

If you're among those with very little equity, you should run some numbers to make sure selling is a realistic option. This is especially important because your mortgage isn't all you'll have to pay off; expect to pay some significant transaction costs when you sell—anywhere from 6% to 14% of the sales price, depending on numerous local factors.

Use the simple worksheet below to calculate how much you can expect to walk away with. Keep in mind this isn't necessarily all "profit"—for example, if you've paid off a significant amount of your mortgage, you'll walk away with more cash, but it will be money you invested, not money you earned. But having some money to use for your next down payment—or at least for your security deposit, if you plan to go back to renting—is an important first step.

To fill out this worksheet, you'll need to know local real estate sales customs. Talking to a local real estate agent or escrow agent about practices in your area is the easiest way to find this out. For example, in some parts of the country, the seller pays for a home inspection, while in other areas, the buyer assumes this cost. Also, find out typical local escrow and attorney fees.

Sales Estimate	
Projected sales price	$
Real estate professional fees (usually 5–6% of sale price)	– $
Other closing costs (such as home inspection, title, survey, escrow, and attorneys' fees)	– $
Liabilities (remaining mortgage obligations, liens)	– $
Total equity	$

If you find, after running the numbers, that you'll end up in the hole when you sell, you have a few choices. If you can afford to make up the difference, you can sell and pay off the mortgage from another source. If you can't, but cutting out agent fees will make a sale feasible, you can try selling on your own, discussed in Chapter 5. (Recognize, however, that buyers might expect you to drop the price a bit if you're not paying an agent's commission, and you'll have some additional expenses, discussed in Chapter 5.) And if selling simply doesn't appear to be a realistic option for you, but you really need to move, you can consider renting your house out (discussed in Chapter 9).

You may have another financial pressure pushing you to make the move—perhaps you've lost your job and can no longer afford the mortgage payments, or your adjustable rate mortgage is about to reset and you can't afford the higher payment. If you think you may be able to pull off a sale at a price that gets you out of the hole, we encourage you to read through all the strategies in this book. But if you truly feel stuck—can't pay the mortgage, and can't sell—look into these options:

- **Refinancing.** Refinancing essentially means you take out a new mortgage. If you qualify to do so (which may be tough and depends on your income, debt load, credit history, and equity in the house), a refinance can help lower your monthly payments in two ways. First, it may lower your interest rate. Second, it will start a new loan term. For example, if you have a 30-year loan for $200,000 and have made payments for five years, you'll probably owe around $186,000. If you kept that loan, you'd have 25 more years to pay off the $186,000. But if you refinance into a new loan term, you'll have 30 years to pay back the money, meaning you'll pay a little less each month. The downside is you'll pay up-front fees to refinance, and pay more interest over the life of the loan, which can cost you thousands of dollars over the years. But if it helps you stay put in the short term, it may be worth it, especially if you think you'll refinance or increase your payments in the future.

- **Negotiating with the lender.** If you've reached the point of having real trouble paying your mortgage, your lender may agree to a repayment plan to help you catch up on missed payments, a modification to your current loan that will make it possible for you to stay put, or a forbearance to reduce or eliminate payments for a period of time, until you're back on your feet. But you'll have to ask first—call, be persistent, and expect to share a lot of financial information to justify why you can't make your payments.

- **Selling in a "short sale."** With a short sale, you will still sell the property, but you get the lender's permission to sell for less than you owe on the mortgage. You won't walk away with any cash, but you generally won't owe the lender anything, either. Lenders sometimes allow this because it can be cheaper than the process of a legal foreclosure, which involves hiring a lawyer, potentially paying an auctioneer or real estate agent directly, or even getting stuck with a property that doesn't sell. If the lender thinks you'll lose the house anyway, this is a money-saving tactic. We'll cover short sales in more detail in Chapter 8.

- **Walking away.** Some homeowners consider walking away from their loan obligations, leaving both the house and the mortgage behind. They reason that there's no incentive to stay if they're just buried in debt. Of course, walking away is perfectly reasonable for people who don't have any ethical opposition to it—some do—and who aren't worried about the effect it will have on their credit. While there's speculation that eventually lenders won't care much about a history of walking away because so many buyers are doing it, for now, it will still make it difficult or impossible—or at least hugely expensive—to get another mortgage.

- **Deed in lieu of foreclosure.** Your lender may be willing to accept a deed in lieu of foreclosure, which means you surrender ownership and the lender takes the property, without the expense of foreclosure (or the harm to your credit).

- **Foreclosure.** If you miss three or four months of mortgage payments, the lender may file a notice of default (legal notice in the public record saying you've defaulted on the loan) and begin foreclosure proceedings, eventually obtaining the right to sell your home out from under you. At the same time, you'll accrue more debt in the form of late and penalty fees, and if you get to foreclosure, you could be stuck with fees for that, too. Your credit will be negatively affected by a foreclosure as well, and you'll likely find it difficult to buy another home for quite some time. All the preceding options are better than foreclosure.

RESOURCE

Find out more about these and other options: See *The Foreclosure Survival Guide: Keep Your House or Walk Away With Money in Your Pocket,* by Stephen R. Elias (Nolo).

Can't Stomach the Low Price? When to Wait Before Selling

If you don't need to move right away, or have a choice about when to sell, figuring out your house's probable selling price inevitably prompts the question: "Can I earn more by waiting?" Many sellers opt to sit tight when the local market is down, hoping for an upswing. Eventually, even if it takes years, the U.S. real estate market always seems to move upward in value.

Before settling on a timing strategy, ask yourself a few questions:

- **How can I make waiting workable?** For example, if your family has expanded, you may want to add on to your current home, which would have the extra advantage of saving the transaction costs of moving. Or if you're changing jobs, you might rent your house out in the short term (as described in Chapter 9), and plan to sell it when the market is stronger.

CAUTION

There are tax consequences for turning your home into a rental. While renting property entitles you to certain tax benefits while you own, it can have a big impact on your taxes when you sell. We'll explain more in Chapter 9.

- **Will waiting make it harder to buy my next house?** If you sell a small home in the hope of buying a larger one in the same community, you may be better off making the transition earlier rather than later. After all, if the value of your smaller house is less than you'd like, the value of the bigger house is probably down, too—and the proportional difference will be greater in a higher priced house.

- **Do I expect the market to improve?** Real estate markets rise and fall. But if you think the market in your area has taken a permanent dip—perhaps because there's a new freeway going up next door, or some other physical blight makes it more permanently undesirable—there's little to be gained from waiting.

- **Can I wait even a few months?** Real estate markets tend to be weakest in cold, dreary winter months (who wants to look at houses in the rain or snow?) and strongest in the spring. If you're trying to unload your house in November, the number of interested buyers is almost sure to be lower than the number in May. Even waiting a few months can make a huge difference. And as we've already described, there's not much point in putting the house on the market in November and figuring spring will come eventually, because the house will appear stale by springtime, and buyers will shy away. ●

Get It in Shape: Preinspections and Repairs

Meet Your Adviser

Paul A. Rude, owner of Summer Street Inspections, based in Berkeley, California (www.SummerInspect.com)

What he does:	Paul is a Certified Member of the American Society of Home Inspectors® who has been inspecting homes in the San Francisco Bay Area since the late 1980s. He also acts as a "remodel coach" for homeowners, helping them avoid trouble with building departments and unscrupulous contractors. As a licensed general contractor, he has done extensive work repairing structural damage, investigating leaks, and upgrading homes for seismic safety. Paul says, perhaps with tongue in cheek, that an inspector's most important qualifications are being nosy and not being afraid of spiders.
Favorite money-saving strategy in tough times:	"Paint stores always have lots of returned paint that's just fine but wasn't the exact color someone else wanted; it's nearly free and even if it's not what you had in mind for the dining room, it will be fine for the basement, garage, or wherever the exact color is not important. If it's a light color, you may even be able to get it retinted closer to what you want. And if you have friends or neighbors whose homes also need sprucing up, put together a cooperative effort—have a painting bee, share a debris box to get rid of junk, and so forth."
Likes best about his work:	"What keeps me going is the satisfaction of helping people understand things that were mysterious to them—such as how leaks can occur due to defects in windows, siding, and trim, even in brand new homes. It's like a teaching profession. People respond, and appreciate the help."

Strangest thing he's seen sellers do: "Leave guns in the closet when buyers are visiting. That really freaks some buyers out. Besides, why risk a buyer stealing one of your guns? And then there were the sellers who left the marijuana-growing hydroponics and lights set up in the attic."

• •

Top tip for homesellers: "Pay attention to the front entry. Make sure the stairs are in good shape, that there's a secure handrail, that the door works properly and is freshly painted or finished, and that the doorbell makes a cheery sound—all of that gives people a good feeling as they enter the house. If you don't have a doorbell or porch light, add them—neither is terribly expensive. And leave the light on in the evenings, even if buyers won't be visiting then. A lot of buyers drive by a house they're considering at night, just to check out the neighborhood. A badly lit house looks gloomy."

The last time anyone took a comprehensive look at your house's condition was probably when you bought it and had a professional inspector write up a report. Since then, you've no doubt fixed and replaced a few things, overlooked some minor problems, and possibly been blissfully ignorant about a few others. It works for you, so why change anything, right?

Maybe—until it's time to sell. Very soon, when prospective buyers come along, they'll be taking a hard look at your home's condition. Obvious issues that a nonprofessional can spot, such as windows with moisture damage around the sills, cracks in the walls and ceiling, and nonworking sinks or electrical outlets can make any home harder to sell. Some buyers may be scared off, thinking you don't take good care of the place and that these small problems are indicative of larger, looming ones. Others will use these problems as negotiating points, perhaps drastically undercutting the asking price to compensate for the cost and trouble of minor repairs.

TIP

The longer you've been in a house, the more problems may have sprung up without your noticing. Adviser Paul A. Rude explains, "Commonly, people have no idea that the roof is worn out and pipes and wires have deteriorated, especially in an older house. It doesn't mean the owner has done anything wrong, it's just that houses age. Another issue that can be very painful is when the owner spent money upgrading the house and there's something wrong with the work—like a defect or code violation. These can be expensive to fix."

Even if you get past the hurdle of minor or obvious problems, if you receive an offer from a serious buyer, it will probably be contingent on having the house professionally inspected and the buyer approving the results. The inspection may turn up a variety of hidden defects or problems. Unpleasant surprises, no matter how small, can again turn the negotiating tables, and not in your favor. In a slow market, a savvy buyer will have lots of other opportunities and knows you aren't in nearly so good a position. The buyer will be thinking, "How much should I take off my offer price for this, without losing this deal?" And if there's any possible reason you could have known about the problem, the buyer may proceed with even greater caution, suspecting that you were trying to pull a fast one.

One step you can take to make sure your house is in the best possible condition—and that a buyer can't take advantage of you later, when problems are discovered during the post-offer inspection—is to do a preinspection yourself. Let's take a look at what you realistically can or should do.

TIP

Live in a planned neighborhood or development? You'll have to work even harder to make sure that your house stands apart from the rest—especially if a number of nearby, similar-looking homes are for sale. Showing that your house has been lovingly cared for can make all the difference.

Root It Out: Inspect It Yourself

Your first step should be to take a walk around the property yourself, looking for problems obvious to the untrained eye. Start with what you know about your home's quirks. For example, you may have gotten used to the broken vertical blinds in the family room, but know that they really need to be replaced. Or perhaps you've learned to walk around a loose floor tile in the kitchen. Fix these, then keep looking around the house to make sure:

- The heating, air conditioning, and water heater work.
- Any appliances that will be included with the house function properly.
- Light fixtures and electrical outlets work properly, no bulbs are burnt out, and there isn't any exposed wire anywhere.
- Flooring and baseboards are not loose or damaged.
- Cabinets and doors are properly hung; sliding doors, latches, and locks function correctly.
- Roof and windows don't leak.
- No cracks are evident in the ceiling or walls.
- There's no water damage to walls, floors, or outside structures.

- Faucets don't leak.
- The toilet doesn't run.
- No mold is growing, anywhere.

Of course, if you discover any problems, you'll need to do something about them: The ideal, if you can afford it, is to avoid the buyer ever witnessing any of them. We'll talk later in the chapter about how to handle repairs; see "To Fix or Not to Fix?," below.

 TIP
Keep manuals, warranties, and repair records for the buyer. Your home appliances and mechanical systems, such as the water heater, built-in microwave, irrigation system, and burglar alarm, should have all come with product manuals or warranties. Don't just recycle these or toss them into a box while moving. Set them aside for your buyer, who will need to know how to handle these things, too. Also pull together records of what's been done on the house. That lets the buyer know, for example, how long ago an item was replaced, or who to call for follow-up work or repairs.

Hire a Professional Home Inspector

If you're serious about making sure your house is in pristine condition, consider hiring a home inspector next. Don't get confused—this isn't the same person who will look at the house later, when hired by a buyer. Instead, this is a pro who works for you, helping identify hidden problems that, if not uncovered until later, let the buyer express shock and horror at your house's "true" state and then start demanding repairs and price reductions. By having your home inspector scout out problems ahead of time, you can either repair them or reduce the price of your home to account for them.

According to adviser Paul A. Rude, "Some real estate agents here in California routinely get a professional inspection done on every house they're preparing for sale." It's less common in other areas, such as New Jersey, where adviser Jaan Henry operates. She says, "I'll go through the seller's house myself and, based on my experience, advise sellers of things to prep, stage, or repair. But if there's any indication that the house might need major structural work, I do recommend that the seller get an inspection— and follow up by getting estimates for the needed work from a couple of contractors, to give to the buyer. (If you wait for the buyer to figure out and negotiate with you over how much the work will cost, you can count on the buyer's own contractors coming in with higher bids.)"

Your own inspection was a good start, of course, but unless you're a contractor or other building professional, you simply won't be equipped to find anything but the more superficial or visible issues, like those mentioned above. By contrast, the most qualified home inspectors are contractors or other professionals with specific knowledge in all aspects of home construction, including plumbing, wiring, and much more.

To find a good inspector, ask friends as well as your real estate agent for recommendations, examine each inspector's sample reports, and make sure the inspector is licensed (if that's required in your state) and is a member of the American Society of Home Inspectors or ASHI (www.ashi.org).

What You Can Ask Inspectors For

For around $250–$700, the inspector will identify problems with the home, such as leaks in the roof, possible water damage, remodeling efforts that don't meet current building codes, and improperly grounded outlets. With this information, the home inspector will prepare a written report and may make repair recommendations. If the report gives your house an A grade (or something close to it), you can hand copies of the report to buyers, to show them what great shape the place is in.

Apart from the general inspection, various specialized types of inspections are available, the most notable being for pests (such as termites, carpenter ants, and dry rot). While some inspectors (usually depending on local custom) mix the pest inspection into the general inspection, these are really two different specialties. Someone who knows foundations doesn't necessarily know termites. So for the most comprehensive inspections, hire two or more different inspectors.

You can also hire inspectors who deal with specialized issues like the condition of your home's soil grading, boat house or other unusual structure, or amenities like a hot tub or swimming pool. But unless you suspect a problem that you're worried a buyer will want to negotiate, you'll probably be okay just hiring a general inspector and perhaps a pest inspector, and letting the buyer decide what other specialists to bring in.

TIP

You may need to give the buyer a pest inspection report. In some areas of the United States, lenders routinely ask to see the results of a pest inspection before they fund the loan. And although it's the buyer who needs the loan, sometimes custom dictates that the seller pay for the pest inspection. A local real estate professional can tell you the practice where you live.

If the cost or hassle of a full inspection is too much for you, hire an inspector who is willing to do a more basic review for less money. Adviser Paul A. Rude says, "Some inspectors, myself included, are willing to do a simple walk-through with the seller, at an hourly rate. (Look for one who's been a general contractor.) It's less comprehensive than a full inspection, and we don't draw up a written report afterward—you'll need to take your own notes—but we'll alert sellers to the major issues. A good inspector will point out which of the home's defects are likely to scare buyers the most and should top the repair list—such as electrical problems, which buyers tend to assume (not always correctly) are a fire hazard, or gutters hanging off, which look shabby. Neither of these are terribly expensive to fix."

Preparing for the Inspector's Visit

You and any co-owners should be present when the inspector comes, especially if you're not going to get a written report. This ensures you retain as much of the information the inspector shares as possible, plus allows you to ask any questions.

You'll get the most from the inspection if you're well prepared. Before the inspector arrives, be sure to:

- **Create a list of issues you'd like the inspector's opinion on.** Even the best home inspectors won't look at each of the hundreds of components of your home. So if there's something you're curious about, like why a light switch won't turn on, bring it to the inspector's attention.

- **Clear any access points.** If there's stuff piled in front of the crawl space entrance or you've forgotten how to open the attic trapdoor, you'll miss your chance to have the inspector examine these areas. Even closets should be cleared out, especially if they're so full it's impossible to access them. Also make sure the inspector can get to the electrical panel.

- **Reread the inspector's contract or brochure.** If you're not sure what's included in the inspection, confirm this with the inspector during the visit. For example, many inspectors won't examine the security system, which you might want to have separately looked at if you suspect a problem.

To Fix or Not to Fix?

Having done your own inspections, and possibly hired an inspector to give you a written or oral report, you now have two choices: You can correct the identified problems, or you can lower your house's sale price to account for them.

What Repairs to Make Right Away

Making certain repairs before you put the house on the market makes sense when they're relatively small and inexpensive, for several reasons. One important reason is that buyers are drawn to a house that's been lovingly cared for, unmarred by a single loose drawer pull or creaking hinge. A small problem left unrepaired has potentially much more impact than it merits, at least in a buyer's mind.

Another reason is that, as mentioned earlier, buyers whose own inspectors discover problems after the sales contract has been signed are likely to negotiate price reductions, especially in a down market when they have good leverage. At worst, the buyer might even cancel the deal if an inspection contingency allows it. As adviser Joel G. Kinney , a real estate attorney in

Massachusetts, notes, "With the market down, we're seeing a lot more jittery buyers. They'll put in an offer hesitantly, then when something comes up, like an inspection issue, use that as an excuse to back out." Adviser Paul A. Rude adds, "It seems to be human nature to forgive problems that are known in advance, but overreact to the same problems after the fact."

A further reason to do repairs ahead of time is that you'll have more control over how they're carried out—and may be able to save some money as a result. For example, while a buyer who discovers loose roof tiles might demand that you hire a professional to replace them, you can replace them in advance yourself, and the buyer will never have to know there was a problem.

Finally, making repairs means you'll have fewer problems to disclose to the buyer. The law in most states requires formal disclosure of known problems, but if you've remedied the problems, you've shortened the list considerably. We'll discuss disclosure requirements further below.

 CAUTION

Don't plan to ignore problems you find during your preinspection. Most state's disclosure laws require you to disclose problems you know about, so the worst possible strategy would be to investigate your house's repair needs but then neither repair them nor tell the buyer about them. If you're not willing to put in the work or notify the buyer, you're better off skipping preinspections altogether.

If you're comfortable handling minor or basic repairs yourself but need a little guidance, look at online websites like thisoldhouse.com, diynetwork. com, or lowes.com. These provide basic "how to" videos and instructions. If you're not equipped to take on these tasks yourself, a general repair person may be able to tackle them for a low cost.

Repairs You Can Probably Handle

Here are some repairs that you can probably handle if you're comfortable using basic tools:

- painting

- coating outdoor woodwork, such as decks

- landscaping, pruning trees, and planting new flowers

- replacing lightbulbs, switchplates, and similar items

- clearing gutters (if the roof isn't too high) and outdoor drains

- changing filters in heating systems

- adjusting or replacing hardware on doors , windows, and cabinets, and

- making basic fence repairs.

The following repairs require more skill, but are still relatively easy with a little advice from your local hardware or home supply store:

- fixing or replacing dripping or otherwise nonfunctional faucets and valves (in many cases, you can turn off the water, remove the item, and take it to a home supply store or plumbing supply house to make sure you get the right parts)

- replacing locks and other hardware on doors

- replacing broken sash cords on windows

- replacing broken parts of irrigation systems

- making minor repairs of concrete sidewalks and masonry

- repairing gates

- adding or replacing spark screens on chimneys, and

- recaulking seams in bathroom floors, around plumbing fixtures, and on the exterior.

> ### Repairs You Can Probably Handle (cont'd)
>
> With a little more preparation and a little greater commitment of time and tools, many people can do these:
>
> - replace vinyl or vinyl tile flooring
> - repair ceramic tile
> - replace cabinets
> - replace worn appliances, such as dishwashers and disposals
> - repair or replace wood siding and trim
> - replace broken window panes
> - replace rusted-out pipes
> - install a sump pump to fix a drainage problem
> - replace a garage door opener
> - install or replace a handrail
> - repair damaged stairs
> - install a drip irrigation system, and
> - refinish wood flooring.
>
> According to adviser Paul A. Rude, "The one area I recommend that homeowners not get into is electrical work, unless they're trained to do it. There's too big a chance of making a mistake that could hurt someone or burn the house down."

Which Repair Needs to Factor Into Your House Price

There are cases when doing a repair before putting a house on the market won't make sense. Major repairs, in particular, like fixing a crack in the foundation, can be very expensive, disrupt your life, and may not even help your bottom line (that is, you won't get $30,000 more for your house because you spent $30,000 repairing the foundation). And the problems may be just plain bigger than you're financially able to handle—for example, if the house needs extensive masonry work on its wraparound brick porch.

In such cases, you may be better off having a contractor take a look and estimate the cost of repair, then lowering the sale price accordingly. You'll then tell prospective buyers that the repair issues exist and were accounted for in the sale price. If a buyer says to you, "I'll pay $10,000 less because there are pieces of defective siding," you can comfortably respond, "I knew about the siding when I researched the price. It's already factored into the market value of the property. It should cost about $2,500 to replace those few pieces, and I listed the house at $3,000 below market value to compensate for that and for any inconvenience to the buyer."

Keeping You Honest: Disclosure Laws

There's a flip side to doing all this inspecting: In most states, you have a duty to disclose known defects to your prospective buyer. If you fix the problem, there's nothing to disclose, but if you don't, you're now under a legal duty to let the buyer know about it. This can be frustrating if you uncover a small problem that feels like more of a headache than it's worth, or the inspector finds something seriously wrong that you had no inkling of.

Got scorpions?

You'll need to disclose them if you live in Arizona, whose disclosure form also asks about rabid animals, bee swarms, rodents, reptiles, and owls. (Owls?!)

But remember, the buyer is likely to have a separate inspection done anyway, especially in a down market where buyers aren't worried about time pressure or competing with other buyers. And unless the buyer happens to choose a completely incompetent inspector, the same repair issues are likely to be revealed.

At that point, you'd be at a psychological disadvantage—at best, the house would appear to be worth less than the price tag you put on it, and at worst, you'd look like you'd been hiding something. Furthermore, in a down market, the buyer is likely to haggle over any and every problem discovered in an inspection. And why not, knowing that you're likely to say yes to paying for repairs, to avoid jeopardizing the whole deal?

The bottom line is that, while seemingly counterintuitive, disclosing your house's problems usually works to your advantage. As adviser and Realtor® Jaan Henry tells her clients, "If you think it's important, or that if it comes out, someone will feel misled, disclose it." And here's one more thought: Even if you can conceal a defect from the buyer and the buyer's inspector doesn't discover it, the buyer may discover it after the sale has closed. At that point, the buyer may well become angry enough to sue you.

Skipping All Repairs: Selling "As Is"

Some sellers who don't want to deal with the hassle of identifying or fixing problems instead think about selling their homes "as is." This essentially says to the buyer, "Here's my house and here's my price; don't expect me to fix anything or lower the price for repairs."

But you can't completely wash your hands of responsibility. Not even an as-is sale relieves you of your duty to disclose the problems you know about. And some buyers will still insist on an inspection contingency in the contract, reasoning that they want to know what the house's problems are before they make a commitment to buy, even if you're not going to fix those problems.

An as-is sale may simplify the sales process, but it probably won't help you get maximum dollar. Interested buyers will expect you to offer a rock-bottom price, to compensate for the risk they're assuming. If there's a major problem with the house, they know it falls entirely on them to deal with it.

In a down market, as-is sales are particularly unprofitable because you're competing with other as-is, low-priced properties, including foreclosures and bank-owned homes. Some of these may be in seriously bad shape, and many buyers will be tired of seeing fixer-uppers. Other buyers will expect your low price to be comparable to the prices on these deeply discounted homes. You're better off fixing your house up and selling it at market value.

> **TIP**
>
> **Don't stop at the fix-ups.** As we'll discuss in the next chapter, savvy home sellers take further steps toward making their homes look gorgeous, by cleaning, decluttering, and adding decorative touches.

Filling Out the Seller Disclosure Form

Most—but not all—states require a seller to give a buyer a written report disclosing the condition of the property and each of its various features. In many states, the law will actually include a standard form for sellers to use. And even in states with no such law, providing written disclosures has become widespread, often using a form prepared by the state's real estate agents' association. In fact, as adviser Nancy Atwood, a real estate broker in Massachusetts (which has no disclosure law) describes it, "If the sellers don't go ahead and provide a disclosure form anyway, most buyers will think they've got something to hide."

Plan to carefully and accurately fill out your seller disclosure form. The form itself will be fairly straightforward. You'll most likely need to answer yes or no questions about, or check off boxes indicating the existence of, various features of the property, such as the roof, foundation, and other structural components; electrical, water, sewer, heating, and other mechanical systems; trees; natural hazards such as earthquakes, flooding, and hurricane; environmental hazards, such as lead, asbestos, mold, and radon; and zoning. You may be asked to rate or describe their condition or to indicate cases where you simply don't know.

Some states' disclosure forms are more comprehensive than others. For example, some go into great detail, even addressing disputes concerning the property, past meth lab usage, or community association fees. Some require information about suicides, murders, and other deaths on the property; nearby criminal activity; or other factors, such as excessive neighborhood noise.

If you really don't know about the condition of certain parts of your property, you're under no obligation to investigate. But if you know about a problem and lie on the form, you may be subject to penalties under state law, and the seller may sue you for fraud or failure to disclose.

A real estate professional in your area, or the state department of real estate, should be able to tell you about the disclosure law in your state and provide the proper form.

Dress Your House for Success: Staging

Meet Your Adviser

Kym Hough, home stager and owner of Staged to Sell in Danville, California (www.staged-to-sell.com) and www.StagersList.com, an online resource for stagers

What she does: As a Certified Staging Professional™, Kym has spent the last six years utilizing her marketing background to help sellers make their homes market ready. The job involves a lot more than matching paint colors, though. On any given job, Kym manages an external team of contractors who may do repair or improvement work, plus her own team, which implements the design-savvy plans she creates to enhance a home's best features.

Favorite money-saving strategy in tough times: "My favorite strategy is a 'green' strategy too, so it's good for the environment. I have placed beautiful tall pots under all of my gutter spouts throughout my yard, so when it rains I capture all of the rain run off from the gutters. I turn off my irrigation system and use this water to water my yard for weeks. It saves fresh water, a natural resource we are running out of, and it saves me money."

Likes best about her work: "I love that every day I get to design a different house—I'm never bored. And I get the instant reward of homeowners oohing and aahing at what I've done. Clients say things like, 'Why didn't I call you five years ago? I would have loved living like this,' or 'Now I don't want to move.' It's satisfying helping people, and it's great hearing that they appreciate it."

Strangest thing she's seen sellers do: "One thing that I see sellers do all the time is put all new appliances in a dated kitchen, before they call me in. I get there and they have spent thousands of dollars on something that may not return their investment. Often it would be better to put in a new countertop, fixtures, and a fresh coat of paint on the cabinets. Then, take a good look at the appliances. The range is a good item to upgrade and if you only have funds for one thing, that should be it. Recently a client put in a new wine cooler in a dated kitchen and left the rest as is … not a good decision."

Top tip for homesellers: "Clean—and that doesn't mean stuffing everything into a closet! Sellers assume buyers only graze the surface, but they're wrong— they open every drawer, cupboard, you name it. Get all your closets in good shape so buyers aren't thinking, 'There's not enough storage space here.' That means moving out at least half of what's in there, making sure the floor of the closet is visible, and color coordinating anything that's hanging—it makes the closet look both organized and larger."

Whether as serious prospective homebuyers or nosy neighbors, we've all walked into open houses and thought, "No way, not in a million years!" It might have been the obnoxiously patterned sofa, the distinct odor of the kitty litter box, or the outdated bathroom vinyl. Even when we're trying, it can be hard to peer through the ugly stuff and clutter to see the potential that lies beneath.

On the other side of the coin, some houses inspire instant "wows" from all who enter. Even in a down market, a well-dressed, sparkling house can attract lots of attention, and potentially sell very quickly. In fact, a down market means buyers don't have to settle for anything less. Why should they spend time and money fixing up a dump when the house down the street, selling at a similarly reasonable price, is move-in ready?

In this chapter, we'll help you evaluate your house's current state and potential, to bring it up to choosy buyers' standards. We'll cover:

- how to stage your home, inside and out
- whether to hire a professional stager
- whether to make major home improvements, and
- how to prep your house for a showing.

Staging Fundamentals

Even if your house is in moderately decent shape, realize that all it takes are a few small distractions to turn off potential buyers. While you've been counting on them to admire the beautiful hardwood floors, they may instead fixate on the smallish coat closet in the living room, or worse, your collection of books or magazines.

Luckily, getting the buyers focused on the right things doesn't mean having to remodel your house. With a little "staging"—that is, an effort to highlight the house's most attractive features—you can get buyers to overlook or concede on some of its less-than-perfect aspects.

What Is Staging?

In the most literal sense, home staging is the act of physically preparing your property for sale. But take a cue from the name—there's a bit of theater involved. You're making your house look its best, so that everyone who comes in imagines living the wonderful life suggested by the stylish yet comfy décor—and hopefully, wants to buy in. Even in a development where homes were built around the same time, with the same or similar designs, a staged home can look fresher, larger, and better maintained than an unstaged one for sale next door.

At the very least, successful staging usually involves a physical makeover: repainting; removing knickknacks and furniture and perhaps replacing existing furniture with a few well-chosen pieces; creating themes and unity for the various rooms (turning a space between the kitchen and garage into an attractive, functional office, for example); using decorative and lighting techniques to draw the eye away from unappealing aspects of the house; then capping it off with a tasteful decor that encourages a variety of buyers to think, "Whoa, this seems like a great place to live."

> ### How discerning are home buyers, really?
>
> A whopping 82% are likely to be distracted from important issues when they go through a staged home—and pay more for it as a result. (Source: 2007 survey by the National Association of Exclusive Buyer Agents (NAEBA).)

It can be hard for sellers to see why staging is a necessity. "I've lived in this house for years and it's perfectly nice looking and comfortable the way it is," you may be thinking. The key is to remember that staging is not about living, but about selling. In the years you've lived in your home, you've probably accumulated a lot of stuff. And you're likely used to your house's little quirks—the bedroom door that doesn't lock, the broken handle on the kitchen cupboard, or the bathroom's 1970s metallic wallpaper.

The problem is, the very things you've stopped seeing are the ones a buyer will likely notice first. You want to make the house appealing to as many people as possible, and that may mean seeing—and changing—unattractive features that aren't even on your radar.

Stage From the Start

If you haven't yet put your house on the market, you must stage it before you do. As you'll learn in this chapter, it's going to take time and money to do it right. Though you may feel like you're losing valuable time by keeping your house off the market in the meantime, look it at this way: One of the main reasons to stage your home is to help it sell quickly. You should ultimately be able to recoup some of that supposedly lost time, because staged homes, on average, take less time to sell.

Also, if you don't stage now, you'll potentially face the same problem we discussed about adjusting your price after initially setting it too high. Your home may sit on the market, with no realistic offers, until the listing eventually becomes "stale." As adviser Kym Hough notes, "The first ten days on the market are critical—when the listing is 'new,' you'll get the most interest and attention. If you don't stage from the start, buyers who visit initially aren't going to come back just to see your great new staging." Even if buyers come around to look again, they'll expect a lower price. You'll really lose both time and money.

Staging Isn't About You

You may still be unconvinced, knowing that your home is already a great place to live. The first step to good staging is realizing that it has absolutely nothing to do with you. Of course your home is a reflection of you and even of your wise choices about what makes a house livable. But prospective buyers want to see an idealized version of themselves, not you, living there. You can help them get there by first removing anything that might make them think of you, then replacing it with an image, scenario, or ambience that will appeal to their vision of a dream future in a dream house.

Another common error people make when staging is assuming that a buyer will appreciate their good taste. While some buyers may love unique features like an elaborate, antique Queen Anne dining table and rose-patterned wallpaper, most won't. Remember your audience: You're trying to attract the most number of prospective purchasers, not hoping for that rare person with similar taste to randomly chance upon your home and fall in love. If your house has a particular architectural style, you should emphasize this attractive feature with furniture and accessories that complement it, but don't go so overboard that your Victorian actually looks like it is from the Victorian age.

Looks Good, but You Won't Enjoy Living in It

Another common source of seller hesitation to staging is that it will be uncomfortable. Indeed, you'll have to hide or pack away a lot of your life's conveniences. "I'm going to hate dragging my toaster out from a cabinet every day," sellers complain. "Why would a buyer even care if it's left out?"

While it's true a buyer might not think, "Hey, there's no toaster on the counter," one might think, perhaps subconsciously, "This kitchen has so much counter space!" The truth is that every little change adds up to create an environment that can make your home more appealing to a buyer. And it's probably going to be inconvenient for you in the short term. But it's precisely because things are so inconvenient—with no relation to everyday living—that they seem so appealing.

> Everyone thinks they have good taste ... but they couldn't all possibly have good taste.
>
> (Marie, *When Harry Met Sally*)

At any rate, living with some short-term inconveniences is better and more cost-effective than dragging out the sale over many months. That could mean having to clean your house neurotically and vacate it at random so potential buyers can look at it, only to finally sell it for less than you could have because it's been languishing on the market. Besides, as adviser Kym Hough notes, "Often families find once they've lived in a staged home for a period of time, they like the clean look and feel and don't miss the clutter. They often go on to live a much less cluttered, easy care life after their staging experience."

Staging a Vacant House

Most of our advice in this chapter assumes that you're still living in your home. If you've already moved, however, don't use that as an excuse to skip the staging.

Vacant houses don't sell well. They feel cold and forbidding and are easily forgotten and rarely hotly desired. Buyers have trouble imagining how a vacant house will look after it's furnished or even how big it really is. They'll instead tend to obsess over details they might not have seen otherwise, like scratches in the floorboards or scuff marks on the baseboards. Worse for your bottom line, the emptiness may telegraph to them that you're paying for a new place and eager to unload this one—perhaps at any price.

A vacant house does, however, give you an opportunity to dress it up without having to conceal your existence there. You can carefully choose pieces of your own furniture and decorative items (if you can spare them or haven't already moved them across the country) with which to make the house look like a home. Borrow or rent the rest. By the time you're done, you may wish you could move back in!

> 💡 **TIP**
>
> **Already buying nice things for your new home?** Whether it's a fresh new throw rug or an antique mirror, consider lending it to your old home if it will help it sell. You can take these things with you later.

Should You Hire a Professional Stager?

Home staging isn't just a technique savvy sellers use to get their homes market ready: it's a career with its own cadre of professionals and related resources. The most highly trained receive a professional designation such as Certified Staging Professional™, but others without this designation (including real estate agents, whom we'll discuss choosing and working with in Chapter 4) may sell you on their staging skills.

Staging professionals have done what you're seeking to do many times before (at least experienced ones—the only kind you want). Their experience will tell them what buyers react positively to. They can come into your space, quickly figure out its problems, and maximize its benefits. And because they're used to specializing in one geographical area, they'll know local tastes and preferences.

A professional stager will (for a fee) give you a written report, explaining what should be done to get the house ready to sell. The written report should go room by room, treating each space as its own. (When interviewing prospective stagers, make sure their services include this kind of report.)

Next, the stager will help you implement the recommended changes. He or she may hire a contractor to replace a dated bathroom vanity, rent you furniture that matches the style of your home, and give you tips on how to clean the place up (or help you find someone to do the cleaning). Because the stager will have many professional contacts, you'll be spared the hassle of finding high-quality professionals or negotiating with them. "Home sellers already have enough to do," says adviser Kym Hough. "A stager helps take away a lot of the stress of preparing a house for the market."

How much will this cost? Hough advises spending roughly 1% to 1.5% of your home's selling price on staging. But as she notes, that should include more than "enhancement staging," making the place look nice. Instead, the stager should be making sure every detail is taken care of—for example, hiring an electrician and making sure new lighting is properly installed. Also, if you were planning to buy new furniture or other items to make the house look good, realize that hiring a stager can be cheaper, because most stagers can provide such items, essentially allowing you to rent them.

TIP

Don't go for the cheapest of the bunch. As with many professional service providers, the cheapest stager isn't necessarily the best. A stager who offers to do the job for less than anyone else may use cheap materials (for example, inexpensive furniture), which won't do as much to sell your home.

Many stagers will work with your budget, too. For instance, they may be willing to do a consultation and provide a report for a relatively small fee—around $250 to $350 is typical. This report will tell you what needs to be done, but allow you to decide whether to do it yourself. Professional stagers also understand that you may not be able to afford some of their recommendations. Just keep in mind that choosing not to make the suggested changes may affect your bottom line.

CAUTION

Don't account for the staging by increasing the price. The stager's job is to make your house better than everything else on the market, so a buyer is drawn to it. If you instead try to capitalize on the staging by charging more for the house, you'll be undoing your competitive advantage.

Choosing a Stager

If you've decided that staging would be a good investment, it's in your interest to choose a stager whose work you like. In many cases, real estate professionals will recommend stagers they've worked with in the past. But you can also get names from friends and neighbors who've sold homes, and visit local open houses and ask who did the staging.

CAUTION

Don't let the agent pay for the stager. Some agents will do so, as a service to their clients. But any money spent on staging will eat into the agent's profit on your sale, giving the agent an incentive to cut corners. Plan on hiring your own stager, so you have control over how much is spent and how.

Once you have a few names, do a little homework, even if your agent made the recommendation. Start by looking up the stager's website. "Web presence is very important," says Hough. "These days, selling a home is a team effort. You want your stager promoting your home, too." For this reason, Hough posts some of her clients' homes on her website, with attractive pictures of the staging—both promoting her work and giving clients some free advertising. Also use the stager's website to evaluate his or her experience and any training or certifications. (The website for the Real Estate Staging Association (www.resa-ho.org) explains some of the available programs.) Finally, expect the website to have some "before" and "after" shots, to show you what the stagers can do.

⊘ TIP

Make your own decision about the stager. Sybil and George, who'd already bought their next home, felt the time pressure of watching the real estate market crash around them while they prepared their first home for sale. They went with the agent's suggestion for a home stager, then were horrified at having to spend money for only slightly varying shades of brown paint on the walls, décor that seemed tacky against their traditional Arts and Crafts bungalow home, and over-the-top touches like champagne glasses on the bedspread. The sale was successful, with more than one offer—but the new owner thought the champagne glasses were ridiculous too, and promptly repainted the brown walls.

Next, call the stagers you're interested in. You may set up an appointment right away, or you may get some of your questions answered over the phone. Ask about experience and cost. (A professional stager won't be able to give you a quote without seeing your home, but should be able to give you a ballpark figure, based on your accurate description of the property.) You can also ask for references of satisfied clients and to see additional photos. Finally, make sure the stager has proper insurance—he or she will be in your home, after all, and you want to know you're protected if someone is injured on the property in the process of staging, or that damage to your home or property (intentional or otherwise) will be covered.

Alternatives to Hiring a Stager

If the expense is inclining you to give up on hiring a pro, you might explore middle-ground alternatives. For example, if you know your house needs to be organized or freed from junk, there's a whole industry dedicated to helping you with just that task. The organizers of the world can give you tips on evaluating, tossing, and sorting everything into neat files and boxes. (Think how much easier your move will be!)

"Most people have a lot of things in their houses that they don't use, but can't agree on what to do with it," says Karen Cabot, owner of Clutter Cutter, a home-organizing business based in Pasadena, California. "A lot of my job is just getting everyone in the household in the same room, to discuss what stays and what goes. Once everyone agrees, the rest goes pretty quickly." To find an organizer near you, visit the National Association of Professional Organizers® (www.napo.net). Look for someone with experience in home organizing (versus office or business organizing).

For more aesthetic issues with your house, you might save money by buying just a few hours of a designer's time. Ask for some general tips about what you can do to make the place look better, and expect answers like, "That corner needs a lamp that directs light toward the ceiling," or "This color is too loud for a small bathroom." You can then implement these changes yourself.

As we've mentioned, some real estate agents will also sell you on their staging skills. We recommend you choose an agent primarily based on real estate expertise and ability to sell your home (discussed in Chapter 4), without expecting too much in the staging department.

Even without the help of others, if you're strapped for cash or simply like the idea of a do-it-yourself (DIY) project, you can do your own staging job. We'll give you advice below on how to pull it off, and there's a plethora of books available on the subject.

DIY Staging Outside: Maximizing Curb Appeal

If you decide to stage your home yourself, the first place to start is outside. The front of your home is the first thing a prospective buyer sees, and some won't even bother to get out of their car if their first impression is negative. Here are some tips for making things look good:

- **Pack up what's going with you.** Pick up any toys, gardening equipment, and debris. If you have a porch, sweep it and clean off any furniture. Get rid of clutter—bye-bye garden gnomes.

- **Spruce up the garden.** Mow the lawn, pull up weeds, and trim the hedges. Pull up any plants that didn't survive the last storm or drought, and trim off dead portions of living plants. If you don't have time to do this yourself, pay someone else to do it (and depending on timing, to maintain it). Make sure you're giving plants enough water, on a regular schedule.

- **Lay out a new welcome mat.** This small (and inexpensive) gesture will make a good impression and keep your floors clean. You can take the mat with you, too.

- **Touch up paint.** If your house is truly in need of an exterior paint job, this can be money well spent. In fact, adviser and broker Jaan Henry says, "This can do more for sales appeal than any other factor." But if the paint just has a few trouble spots—peeling around the windows, for example—you can just do a simple touch up. Also consider painting the door and window trim—these small accents will have big impact.

- **Wash windows and siding.** Cleaning the windows will make a big difference both inside and out, freshening the appearance of your home and letting in more natural light. You can wash screens or take them down (store them in the garage). Also make sure the driveway and sidewalk are clean (a pressure washer works well) as well as the external siding.

- **Get rid of cobwebs or signs of other pests.** Cobwebs, for example in the corners of your porch ceiling and around windows, make a house look unkempt. Spray for spiders in those areas around your home if you have problems; this will prevent them from reappearing.

- **Clear downspouts and gutters.** Even if it's the middle of summer, clean gutters look neater and show that you take good care of your home.

- **Plant new plants.** Some new, blooming foliage might brighten things up. A potted plant on either side of the front door adds a cheerful touch and is easy to care for (if the plants die, you can quickly replace them). Plus, unless the planters are so big as to be considered "fixtures," you can take them with you when you move.

- **Make sure the house is well lit.** First off, buyers need to be able to see your house number. Make sure it's clearly visible, and repaint or replace it if necessary. Then step outside and check whether all the other lovely features of your home can be clearly seen, at any time of day or night. Many buyers drive by at night, and it's also a good idea to have an attractive evening shot on your website. Consider putting outdoor lights on a timer that goes on automatically, or buy inexpensive solar lights for a walkway or landscaping.

- **Get rid of old cars.** Buyers are put off by clunkers in the driveway.

The backyard won't control the buyer's first impression, but it's arguably just as important. That's because it's a functional space—buyers will look forward to treating it like another room, especially in warmer climates. Do the same kind of clean-up you did in the front, making sure everything is in working order.

If the backyard space doesn't already appear to be useful for something other than staring at from the kitchen window, take steps to make it so. If you don't have a back deck or patio area, consider whether you can alter the space to create that illusion—for instance, by placing a patio table on the lawn and surrounding it with lights and potted plants. If you don't have a patio table, consider buying or borrowing one. It doesn't need to be anything fancy, but it does need to convince a buyer that the back deck is a perfect place for a summer meal. You can get budget ideas for a simple patio on do-it-yourself websites like hgtv.com or diynetwork.com.

DIY Staging Inside: First, the Basics

Leave some time to work on the inside of your house—it's usually even more important to buyers than the outside. Before you can even think about aesthetic touches for different rooms, you'll need to do some crucial preparation work.

Declutter

Decluttering sounds easy in theory: Most people understand that their unused stuffed animal collection isn't universally appealing and can be boxed up. But decluttering is much more than that. Here are some specific guidelines:

- **If it's just to look at, it's not necessary.** Artworks and knickknacks are not automatically clutter—a simple print can enhance a blank wall, for example—but you should look at each one and decide whether it adds aesthetic value. If not, pack it up and enjoy it in your new home.

- **If you haven't used it in six months, pack it up.** If you've lived six months without the immersion blender you bought at a garage sale or your kids no longer play with the race track they got for Christmas, you can certainly put those away for now.

- **You need less than half the clothes in your closet.** Box up seasonal items and things you don't wear, shoes included. When in doubt, try your clothes on. For most people, this eliminates about half of what's there, if not more. Make sure what's remaining looks neat and well organized, all nicely folded, hung, or arranged.

- **Take out a third of your furniture—no exaggeration.** Start with the obvious: bookcases (the books can easily be stored), footstools that are convenient but take up space, and a china cabinet in an already overcrowded dining room. In the short term, you'll hardly miss them.

- **Make it light and bright.** If your house looks lighter, it will also look bigger and cleaner. You can create this illusion by making sure all blinds and curtains are open and also by using indirect artificial lighting, such as track lighting or lamps that point upward. But, avoid powerful fluorescent bulbs, which look institutional. (Of course, you'll want to save your eco-friendly compact fluorescent lightbulbs (CFLs) and use them again after the house is sold.) Also make sure the wattage is high enough—a mere 20-watt bulb in the bathroom, for example, will make it look dark and dreary.

TIP

Swap out any fixtures you want to take with you. The buyer has a right to keep all fixtures, or items permanently attached or affixed to the property, such as lights, curtains, and built-in appliances. But it's still your house, and there's no law against replacing fixtures before the buyer ever sees them. If you know that you'll want to use those silk curtains or trusty stove in your new home, trade them out now—before the buyer has a chance to assume they come with the house. Of course, your replacements should be attractive and preferably new, even if you pay less for them than you did for the original fixtures.

- **Pretend you're living in a vacation rental.** If you've ever rented a cabin, it probably came with the bare minimum: one corkscrew, one frying pan, one set of towels. Its sparseness may have been inconvenient, but you made do. Emulate that to make your house—including your cupboards, closets, and storage spaces—feel larger.

TIP

Don't just shift everything to the garage or closet. Buyers won't hesitate to open doors and examine these spaces. And if any are over-full, they may think "Oh, not enough storage." Better to spend a little to rent a storage space, transportable storage (check out PODS at www.pods.com), or barter for space with family or friends.

Depersonalize

As mentioned above, the fewer clues you leave that a specific person lives in your home, the easier it will be for a buyer to imagine living there. Depersonalizing isn't just about removing literal images of you and your family, however. To erase your own influence, you should:

- **Hide personal photographs.** Remove photos on the wall or, in bare spots, replace them with simple prints (think photographs or paintings of attractive but forgettable locations, flowers, or the like). Also get rid of friends' Christmas photos, postcards, or baby announcements on the refrigerator or mantle.

- **Eliminate pet smells and effects.** It's hard to neutralize the effect of pets in your home, but do your best. Make sure there's no dog bowl in the kitchen or kitty litter box in the bathroom, and if possible, get your pets out of the home for every showing. (That means out of the yard, too. Your dog's barking may mean, "Hello!" but buyers may hear it as, "Go away or else!") If your pets will be there, contain them as best you can, and make sure your listing notifies others (mention the pet's name, so the agent or prospective buyers don't startle the animal).

TIP

Ask friends for their honest opinions. It can be difficult to be objective about your own space. But friends will immediately point out things you were blind to, for example if you ask them, "If you were thinking of buying this house, what would be tops on the list of things you don't like?" Emphasize that your feelings won't be hurt. You might even hold a mini "open house" for neighbors or friends to share these perspectives and give feedback.

- **Get rid of other strong odors, too**. When you first step into your house after being away for several hours, put it through the sniff test. You may want to use neutralizing sprays in the kitchen and bathroom. If you're a smoker, start stepping outside to light up, store the ashtray out of sight, and throw away any butts.

- **Remove distinct artwork, décor, and collections.** A spoon collection is more than just clutter, it's a statement about you and what you value or spend your time doing. You don't want the buyer to be able to tell anything about you personally.

- **Neutralize color.** Paint color is the most logical and inexpensive place to start—go for warm but neutral shades. Also remove or replace any clashing accent pillows, towels, curtains, or other decorative accessories.

> *Want proof that most people love neutrals?*
>
> Check out Benjamin Moore's top-selling paints at www.myperfectcolor.com. Just select "Top Selling Paint Colors" from the menu on the left, and see for yourself— there's hardly a bright color in the bunch.

- **Put away signs of religion, politics, or ideology.** It may seem silly, but get rid of books or paraphernalia that are political or religious in nature. No sense alienating prospective buyers whose views differ from yours. Similarly, if you have any paraphernalia that speaks to a potentially polarizing view—the legalization of marijuana, for example—stash it away for now.

Clean up

When you show your home, it must be spotless. This not only makes the space look its best, it suggests that you take good care of it. You may already think you keep things pretty clean. But lots of the dirt in your home may be invisible to you: the dust that accumulates on the top of ceiling fans, the gunk that's growing in the back of the cabinet under the sink, the grime that builds up on the windowsills. Go over the place with a fine-tooth comb. Also polish any hardware, such as brass faucets and doorknobs.

If you're not feeling up to the task, hire someone else to do an initial deep clean. This may cost you a couple hundred dollars, but it will ensure things are in great shape to start. Of course, it will be up to you to keep it up.

If you do the cleaning yourself, start in one room and work your way through methodically. This will help you focus on one task at a time and keep you from missing something.

TIP

First declutter and depersonalize—then clean. It will be easier to thoroughly clean with less in the way. Besides, you may make a mess sorting through all your stuff, so why clean it up twice?

Staging, Room by Room

Though each room must be cleaned, depersonalized, and decluttered, different rooms call for specific treatment. Here are some easy, inexpensive (mostly free!) ways to make each room look its best. And even after you're done implementing our tips, take a last look at each room to see whether it has a cohesive look. Then add finishing touches—for example, by setting the dining room table to look like a dinner party is about to happen. This can help create a positive focal point, drawing buyers' eyes to the room's best features (but don't overdo it—just one faux party at a time is enough).

RESOURCE

Get ideas from photos of professional stagers' work. Many stagers' websites include before-and-after pictures, which are great for seeing how an uninspiring space can be transformed. Search for "home stager" or check the websites of stagers recommended by your friends and real estate agent.

Kitchen

The kitchen is one of the home's most important rooms—one that buyers will take a close, long look at. Here are some tips for making yours look great:

- **Remove all appliances from the countertop.** Box up ones you use only occasionally and can get away without; put the rest under the counter. Same for dish soap, sponges, and the rest.

- **Pack away dishes or other items you use only every once in awhile.** Also get rid of extras—you can probably get by with six wineglasses instead of 12 for the next few months, for example.

- **If you have tile, clean the grout.** Over time, it gets stained. A solution of bleach and water should restore its color.

- **Clean the oven.** It's no one's favorite job, but buyers will look.

- **Wipe down and oil the front of cupboards.** Get rid of the inevitable built-up grease and dirt. If you have wood cupboards, use lemon or orange oil to restore their sheen.

What do your kitchen cabinets say about you?

According to kitchen cabinetmaker Merillat, there are four types of kitchen users:

Luxury Leaders, who want their kitchens to reflect their social status

Domestic Dwellers, who see the kitchen as a family gathering place and want something low maintenance

Busy Bees, who multi-task in the kitchen, and want to improve efficiency and cut clutter

Career Builders, who spend more time working than at home and care more about resale value than usability

Source: National Association of Realtors®

- **Put the garbage can out of sight.** This will make the place look cleaner and reduce any smells. Adviser Kym Hough recommends putting the garbage in the garage, not just under the sink, to remove possible odors from the house.

- **Clean out the fridge.** Reduce the number of condiments and get rid of anything that's moldy. Wipe down the shelves.

- **Wipe down the walls.** Over time, they get grimy, especially the spot over the stove. The range hood may need a good grease cutter, too—vinegar works well. Ceiling or vent fans may also need special treatment.

- **Change shelf liners.** This will keep the inside of your cupboards looking fresh and clean.

- **Get rid of kitchen kitsch.** If you have knickknacks or a cute decorating theme—country old-fashioned, for example—it's time to downplay it. The kitchen should be a fairly neutral room, with the clean, welcoming look of a place where anyone would like to prepare a meal.

- **Fill a bowl with fruit.** Nothing looks homier than food. A filled-up, glass cookie jar or a fresh-baked pie are also warm touches.

Bathroom

The bathroom is another place where buyers will pay particular attention. It should feel clean, spacious, even reminiscent of a spa. Here are a few ways to make that happen.

- **Buy new, matching towels in a neutral color.** Even if you currently have neutral-colored towels, new ones will look luxurious and inviting. Don't use these towels, either. Keep the ones you're actually using out of sight, perhaps temporarily stored in your dryer.

- **Change out the shower curtain.** Especially in a small bathroom, a light-hued, solid color, fabric shower curtain makes the space feel large and luxurious.

- **Add a handful of decorative accessories.** The bathroom counter is a bad place to store personal hygiene products, but a great place for a vase of fresh flowers or a pretty candleholder. You can also use these small decorative items to add a little color to complement the neutral tones in the room.

- **Clean the vent fan.** It tends to accumulate dirt over time and may be something you rarely notice since it's not in your direct line of sight.

- **Check for mold or mildew in the shower.** This is an automatic and loud turnoff; it suggests there may be more mold lurking elsewhere. Bleach and water should do the trick. Also check the ceiling, especially over the shower.

- **Store all toiletries in a cupboard.** Keep the countertops clear of these necessities.

- **Clean out the medicine cabinet.** Get rid of old prescriptions that you don't use. (While you're at it, hide the rest of your prescriptions: Open-house visitors have been known to steal painkillers and other widely used medications.)

- **Keep it simple in the shower.** You really need only one bottle of shampoo and conditioner and a bar or bottle of soap. Store these under the sink to give the shower a fresh look.

- **Set out a dispenser of liquid hand soap.** This is less messy than bar soap. If you have more than one sink, buy matching dispensers. Spring for a luxury brand with a pleasant scent such as lavender.

- **Clean out the drain.** Drains clog and slow down with a steady, often unnoticeable, accumulation of hair and soap residue. An easy, natural way to keep your drain maintained: Pour in a cup of baking soda, a cup of salt, and a cup of vinegar (don't premix this, put it right in the drain itself—otherwise you'll have a mini-volcano on your hands!). After 15 minutes, follow with some boiling water.

Living or Family Room

This is where people envision spending most of their communal time. You can make it look like a good gathering spot using these tips:

- **If possible, get the TV out of sight.** At the very least, make sure it's not turned on while a buyer is visiting.

- **Clear a pathway through the room.** Arrange furniture so that it's comfortable not only to sit and talk in, but to walk around.

- **Brighten up "dead" corners.** If a corner is unoccupied, consider putting a floor lamp there. Or buy large potted plants that will naturally make the corner look lush and inviting.

- **Keep it simple.** Make sure the room hasn't become a multipurpose "pool table, art projects, and bike storage" room.

- **Get rid of oversized furniture.** If at all possible, remove bulkier pieces like an oversized sofa or armchair; they just make the room look smaller. If you can't avoid large pieces—for example, your sofa is the only place to sit in the room—at least get rid of accents that make the piece look even more imposing, like throw pillows or blankets.

- **Make colors match.** If you have a yellow couch that clashes with your green chairs, offset by a purple rug, you'll confuse and overstimulate the buyer's senses. Either cover or remove furniture or accessories that don't match. A slipcover can be an inexpensive yet effective option for updating an old couch, too.

- **Decorate the walls.** You don't want walls that are totally bare. While it's a good idea to take down your family photos, don't leave huge blank spots. Choose two or three tasteful photographs or prints, in frames, to deal with the barest walls.

- **Dress up the fireplace.** If you have a fireplace, it can make a great focal point to your living room. But if the screen has gotten dusty or torn, hide it (or at least wash and repaint it). Many stagers now replace the screen with an eye-catching new one. Also scrub the bricks or tiles, sweep out ashes, and put fresh logs on the fire.

TIP

If you don't have the right furniture, you can rent it. Your best bet may be to call local stagers, who often rent furniture at reasonable prices. You can also try rental companies near you, or visit Cort Furniture (www.cort.com). If a friend or family member has the right item, you may even be able to borrow it—or exchange it, perhaps for a nice meal out or a night of free babysitting.

Bedrooms

Bedrooms are places to sleep, but they're more than that—they're havens for each member of the family to personalize and design for comfort. Here are some ways to make these rooms appealing to buyers.

- **Don't hide your clutter under the bed.** If buyers look there, they'll instantly be wise to your scheme.

- **Buy new linens.** You can inexpensively brighten and freshen your space by putting a new cover on the bed and adding a couple of attractive and well-coordinated pillows. Make sure the bed cover matches nicely with everything else in the room too, like your curtains, rug, and walls.

- **Stick to basic furniture.** You don't need much more than a bed, side tables, and a dresser. If those items are big and bulky, consider removing or replacing them. You may even be able to create replacements yourself—you can get ideas for how to make a simple headboard at hgtv.com (search "headboard").

- **Don't use master bedrooms as multifunctional spaces.** Master bedrooms are considered havens today—spaces for relaxing or sleeping, not working, watching television, or paying your bills. Make sure your room looks like a getaway from regular life. In particular, take the desk or television set out.

- **Get rid of large kids' toys.** Large plastic toys in loud colors are particularly unattractive. Have kids choose a handful of their favorite toys, then pack the rest away for the next house.

- **Gender-neutralize children's rooms.** As much as you can, make children's rooms universally appealing. A pink canopied bed or one in the shape of a race car screams girl or boy; it will be harder for someone with a child of the opposite gender—or no child at all—to see beyond this.

> **TIP**
>
> **Get the kids involved.** Adviser Kym Hough recommends talking to your kids about the temporary changes and regular cleanups that are part of selling your home. "I ask my clients, 'What kind of incentive can we give your kids here?' Whether it's a new toy for packing away less-frequently used toys or a special privilege for pitching in to clean the bathroom every day, you may find the process easier if your kids are committed to it."

- **Make sure teenagers keep their rooms clean.** Also take down the ubiquitous posters—bands, heartthrobs, or otherwise. Your teens can always reintroduce these in the next house (if their loyalties or obsessions haven't already changed).

- **Don't use bedrooms as lifestyle rooms.** You may have turned an extra bedroom into a craft room, football paraphernalia room, or children's playroom—but most buyers won't be interested in those uses. If you have extra bedrooms, you can convert one to an office. Otherwise, make sure bedrooms are set up to accommodate as many people as are likely to be in your typical buyer's family.

- **Put the hamper in the closet.** This goes for the diaper pail too; and make sure it's a smellproof one like the Diaper Genie.

- **Keep the bedside tables clear.** Get rid of the usual clutter—your reading glasses, glass of water, or bottle of hand lotion, for example.

- **Straighten out the closets.** After clearing out all the "extras," make sure all the hangers are facing the same way, your shoes are neatly paired, and everything on shelves is carefully stacked.

> **TIP**
>
> **Don't stop there!** Every room in your house deserves at least some attention in the staging process. For example, adviser Jaan Henry suggests, "Clean out your basement, attic, and garage and stack boxes neatly near—but not against—the wall. (You need to leave space for the pest inspector's examination.) If your basement is dark and gloomy, consider painting the walls and ceiling a light color. And vacuum even the garage floor and rafters."

Home Improvements: Are They Worth It?

How far should you go in preparing your house for sale? You may be convinced that better lighting, new flooring, or a brand new countertop (all the things you meant to add when you lived there) will help you sell quickly.

That may be true, but proceed with caution. Major home improvements don't always result in a significantly higher sale price—at least, not enough to recoup their cost. Even the most valuable home improvements, like kitchen and bathroom remodels, rarely pay for themselves when you sell. If you're considering doing a remodel or making a major improvement, see *Remodeling Magazine*'s "Cost Versus Value" report, an annual publication that estimates what percent of a project you'll make up when you sell (find it at www.remodeling.hw.net).

That's not to say that a remodel or improvement before selling never makes sense. Here are a few occasions when it's worth considering:

- **You're selling a high-end home.** If you're in a neighborhood of multi-million dollar homes, spending $20,000 to upgrade a bathroom may be recouped when you sell. It's far less likely to have that level of impact in a $300,000 house, however.

- **You're making your home conform with the rest of the neighborhood.** If you live in a neighborhood of other homes that have been upgraded, and your upgrades will simply help your house look like everyone else's, it will become easier to accurately price your home consistent with the neighborhood. (But make sure the price of comparable remodeled homes isn't too low to justify the cost of remodeling.)

- **You're making one room in your home conform with the rest.** If you've updated everything but one bedroom, which still has old wallpaper and carpet, it will stick out like a sore thumb. Even a small investment to replace the wallpaper and carpet will have a huge impact, making the room "fit in" with everything else.

- **You can turn dead space into functional space.** You may have space in your house that can be transformed into something buyers want—for example, by turning a half bath into a full bath.

In general, if you decide to make any improvements, you'll get the most for your money if those improvements are visible to buyers. For example, while upgrading electrical wiring in an older home makes it safer and therefore more desirable, it doesn't excite buyers' imaginations. But a remodeled kitchen or new hardwood flooring is right before their eyes, looking great.

Ta Da! Finishing Touches Before a Showing

After all your hard work, you want to make sure the house continues to look good when a prospective buyer comes along. Here are some tips for doing that:

- **Keep a bottle of all-purpose cleaning spray handy in the kitchen and bathroom.** You can do a quick wipedown at a moment's notice.

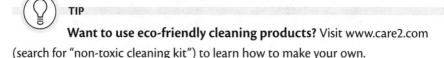

TIP

Want to use eco-friendly cleaning products? Visit www.care2.com (search for "non-toxic cleaning kit") to learn how to make your own.

- **Use microfiber cloths to combat dust and debris.** These handy cloths are particular good for dusting wood surfaces or picking up stray pet hairs from a hardwood or other solid-surface floor.
- **Open curtains and turn on the lights.** This helps everything look bright and spacious. If a room still looks dim, consider taking down heavy curtains or blinds.
- **Get everything off the counters.** In the kitchen, put it neatly in the dishwasher; in the bathroom, store it under the sink.
- **Make sure the beds are made and no clothes are lying around.** Keep a hamper in the closet, or immediately throw everything into the washing machine (you can run it later).
- **Vacuum.** A regular biweekly schedule will help keep things in good order, but you may need to do a touchup on those little dust bunnies.
- **Empty the trash.** It looks neater and avoids unattractive smells.

- **Clean the windows.** No time to do each window? Wipe down the ones that let in the most light or any trouble spots, like the sliding glass door where your dog's nose leaves smudge marks. A mixture of vinegar and water works very well.

- **Make it smell pleasant.** A neutral and consistent aroma around the house—no strong fruit or flower smells, which some people will not like—creates a comfortable ambience. An odor-neutralizing spray may do the trick.

- **Turn on some gentle music.** Jazz or classical is usually best. Keep the volume low enough to be unobtrusive, but just high enough to create a relaxed mood and mask outdoor traffic or other noises.

- **Arrange flowers.** These don't need to be giant, expensive bouquets. But nothing dresses a house up more effectively than an artful selection of blooms. Even a single rose in a vase looks nice in an entryway or windowsill. Ask your florist for suggestions for long-lasting and not too heavily fragrant flowers. Another favorite method stagers use to bring life to a house is a big bowl full of fresh lemons and limes.

- **Set the right temperature.** You don't want buyers to feel too hot in the summer or too cold in the winter, so set the thermostat accordingly. If you have a fireplace, you may want to light a fire if it helps set the mood—for example, on a rainy winter afternoon.

- **Look at which car is parked in front.** If it's your teenage son's flashy hot rod or a visiting uncle's gnarly old pickup with torn-off fenders, ask them to move it to the next block.

Get the Best of the Best:
Hiring a Real Estate Professional

Meet Your Adviser

Mark Nash, an associate broker with Coldwell Banker, who serves the Chicago, Evanston, Skokie, and Wilmette areas of Illinois (www.marknashrealtor.com)

What he does:	When Mark's not working with homebuyers or sellers, he shares his expertise through books, articles, and media interviews. Among his many books, you'll want to check out *1001 Tips for Buying and Selling a Home*, which the Library of Congress actually invited him to come to Washington, DC and make a presentation about. Mark has toured thousands of homes in his career as a Realtor® and as a real estate investor.
Favorite money-saving strategy in tough times:	"I actually keep track of every cent I spend, in business and in my personal life. Whether it's a marketing cost, like taking someone to coffee, or a personal expense, like going out to dinner and a movie, I've figured out that the best way to save money is to see where you spend it. And having a budget helps keep me on track—it's like a diet, if you fall off the wagon, you feel guilty."
Likes best about his work:	"The people part. For me, real estate is more about people than houses."

Strangest thing he's seen sellers do: "A frustrated couple had a temper tantrum when they got a lowball offer. This was in July 2007, in a market that was transitioning. These sellers had resisted being properly priced, believing their house was special. After it sat for a few months, I got them to reduce the price. We got three offers in three days, all within $10,000 of each other but much less than what they'd asked for, which infuriated them. They kept screaming on the phone 'This isn't fair!' I explained, 'We don't decide this. This is the market speaking, telling you this is the price at which your house is going to sell. It's not about fairness, it's about value.'"

* *

Top tip for homesellers: "Be realistic and be patient. Learn how to read the tea leaves as they change. Sold comparables are the key—the market's shifting so fast that the six months rule is changing. Sellers really need to look at the last 60 days for the truest indicator of a realistic sales price. And it's important because even if you find a buyer willing to pay a price comparable to one for sale six months ago, mortgage lenders are getting more and more strict in their appraisals. Lots more deals are falling apart at that stage. I tell my clients, buckle your seatbelts as tight as they've ever been, then tighter. There's going to be plenty of turbulence, and you won't have any idea of when to unbuckle."

Selling a house isn't something you do every day, and there's a lot at stake, especially in a down market. Pricing errors, lax marketing, failure to distinguish the strong offers from the weak—all of these can undermine your ability to sell your house quickly and for the best possible price.

It's during times like these that it's nice to have a professional working alongside you, to make sure you get things done right. And fortunately, there are plenty of those professionals at the ready. They go by various names: real estate agent, real estate broker, or in the case of someone who's a member of the National Association of Realtors® (NAR), Realtor®. A good agent is many things at once: a confident salesperson, marketing guru, organizer, negotiator, creative thinker and problem solver, and just plain hard worker.

Of course, you don't get all that for free. In fact—and this can be tough to swallow in a down market—one of your biggest expenses in selling will be paying the agent. The standard payment method is by commission, typically 5% to 6% of the home's selling price. Your agent doesn't pocket the full amount; it's usually split in half with the buyer's agent, and then your agent divvies up what's left with the broker (the agent's boss). Also, your agent bears many of the costs of marketing your property, which can be significant. The bottom line is that you want to hire an agent whose high-quality work will justify the commission.

In this chapter, we'll explain:

- reasons to hire an agent
- how to choose an agent, and
- how to hire an agent and negotiate the commission.

SKIP AHEAD

Wondering whether you can save money by selling without an agent? It's possible, but not always practical. We'll discuss the pros and cons of selling "FSBO" (for sale by owner) in the next chapter.

Why Hire an Agent?

Before you get too focused on the commission you'll pay for an agent's services, realize one thing: Good agents do a lot of work to earn their commission, saving you time and energy, and hopefully getting your house sold quickly and for more money. The main tasks they'll handle include:

- **Setting the list price.** As we discussed in Chapter 1, setting the right price is a must from the get-go. If you overprice, you risk your house sitting unsold for weeks or even months, until no one wants to look at it anymore. If you underprice, you lose money. With access to important market information, agents will know how to hit the right balance. They've done it many times in the past (hopefully, in your neighborhood).

> *Are you overly optimistic about your house's worth?*
>
> A Coldwell Banker report showed that more than three-quarters of the real estate agents it surveyed said most sellers set unrealistically high list prices for their homes.

- **Helping you prepare the house for sale.** Ultimately, getting your house ready for sale will be largely up to you (your real estate agent can't literally force you to clean or pack up clutter, for example). But your agent will have enough experience to offer information and advice about what needs doing and how to make the house look its best, having staged or prepared many homes for sale in the past.

- **Advertising the property for sale.** A big factor in getting your house sold is making sure as many buyers as possible know it's on the market. Your agent may advertise by posting online, carrying out mail campaigns, doing open houses (both for other agents and for the public), and more. For marketing ideas, see Chapter 7.

- **Screening prospective buyers.** When interested buyers want to look at your house or get more information, they'll call your agent, not you.

- **Showing the property to prospective purchasers.** Your real estate agent may walk prospective buyers through your home privately as well as at open houses.

- **Ensuring buyers receive proper disclosures.** Your state may require you to disclose certain known problems with your home to prospective purchasers. Additionally, you may be required to make certain environmental disclosures—for example, if your house is old enough, a disclosure that it may contain lead-based paint. And your city may add other requirements to the mix—for example, whether there have been any deaths on the property. Your agent will explain what information you must provide, and will probably give you a standard form or set of forms that meet legal requirements.

- **Reviewing offers and negotiating a deal.** When someone offers to purchase your home, your agent will review the offer with you, explain any confusing spots, give you advice on the strength of the offer, suggest what to ask for or concede, and explain any problems or areas of concern. Then, the agent will work with the buyer's agent to iron out the terms of the deal, protecting your interests in the process.

- **Making sure everything gets wrapped up by the closing date.** Once you and the buyer have reached an agreement, you'll have to make sure all the steps leading up to the closing (during what's called the escrow period) are properly completed. An important part of this will be making sure that all contract contingencies are met and released by the dates stated in the agreement. That may involve, for example, making your house available for inspections, and following up by arranging for repairs. Your agent will work with you, the buyers' agent, and the closing agent to coordinate all this.

Finding and Choosing a Top-Notch Agent

You've probably heard or read that the real estate market is flooded with agents. Critics of the burgeoning industry have some valid concerns: Getting a real estate license is fairly easy to do (unlike in many other professions), which means there are many unskilled agents out there. Some agents enter the market only part-time, making it difficult for their customers to work with and rely on them. And the plethora of agents makes it difficult for the unknowing consumer to distinguish the good ones from the bad.

The good news is, in a slow market, the less-serious and less-qualified agents often give up the profession. They simply can't make enough money to stay afloat. Still, you may find a surprising number of agents vying (in some cases, desperately) for your business. You'll need to invest some time in finding the best.

Why You Must Choose Carefully

Remember, you pay the same commission to an agent whether you get horrible service or wonderful service. While one agent may be willing to spend long hours aggressively marketing your house, another may be planning to do no more than post its description on the local MLS website and let it sit. The point is, hiring a real estate agent makes financial sense if you hire a *good* agent, one who will actively help you sell your house, and quickly. A good real estate agent is a bargain, because you won't pay a penny more than you would have for a lousy one.

Of course, you can't just ask someone, "Are you a good agent?" Later in this chapter, we'll give you a list of specific questions you can ask prospective agents to help elicit this important information. You're looking for an agent with experience (at least a few years as a residential real estate agent) and education (such as professional courses and certifications). But you should seek out other characteristics as well: someone who is trustworthy, personable (you'll be working together a lot, plus counting on the agent to get along well with buyers), and flexible and able to adapt to challenging market conditions. And above all else, you're looking for results: an agent with a proven track record of getting homes sold in the tough market you're in.

What's the Difference Between an Agent and a Broker?

When you're out searching for an agent, what you're really looking for is a real estate salesperson. Technically, that person may either have a salesperson's license or a broker's license. At a minimum, a salesperson's license is needed to represent you in a real estate transaction; a broker's license means the individual has undergone additional training.

Many real estate agents have a broker's license, but don't act as managing brokers. The managing broker is the person in a real estate office who supervises other real estate salespeople. When you sign a listing agreement with your agent, you'll probably need the approval of the managing broker.

You'll probably never meet the managing broker. However, if you have problems with your agent, or if your transaction is particularly complicated, the managing broker may get involved. He or she will also take a cut of the commission you pay—most likely, half of what your agent gets.

Getting Names of Recommended Agents

Getting the best agent will likely involve more targeted activity than calling up the first name you find through a search engine or see on a billboard. Instead, you'll want to rely on other people to get started.

First off, you probably worked with an agent when you bought your home. That may be the first person you call, if you liked working together. If the agent works only with buyers, he or she should at least be able to recommend respectable seller's agents. Alternatively, if you were impressed with the seller's agent, that may be the logical place to start.

Second, ask friends, colleagues, and neighbors for the names of agents they've worked with. Make sure they're not just giving you their cousin or a good friend, however—you're really only interested in professional recommendations, based on actual experiences. Neighbors are a particularly good bet, since any agents they've worked with should know the area well. Some may be able to offer only the names of people they *don't* recommend, but that can be helpful too—you can narrow down your list, especially if you get more than one negative report on the same agent.

Next, consider contacting local professionals in related fields, such as your accountant or attorney. They've probably worked with real estate professionals in the past and may have good recommendations.

Finally, if you don't have anyone to ask for recommendations, you can go to your local, state, or national association of Realtors® for a few names. If you take this approach, we recommend interviewing at least three or four agents, to give you a range of options. You may even want to discuss some of the preliminaries on the phone, just so you don't waste your time with agents you're not really interested in.

Showing a Prospective Agent Your Home

Eventually, you're going to sit down with prospective agents and go through a detailed list of questions to help you select the right one to sell your home. But first, you'll allow the prospective agents to *see* that home.

At your initial meetings, the agents will most likely come over and take a peek. They'll use what they see to help create the comparable market analysis (CMA) we talked about in Chapter 1. They'll want to look at your home's specific features, so as to compare them to those of other homes. No two houses are exactly alike, and upgrades or special features your house has that comparable properties don't can raise its value (or vice versa).

Evaluating the Agent's Presentation

Once the agent has taken a good look at your place (and assuming you like what you've seen of the agent so far), it's time to arrange another meeting. At that meeting, you'll ask the interview questions below, plus get the CMA that the agent has compiled in the meantime.

The CMA should include all properties sold in the last six months that are truly comparable to yours—that is, similar in size, location, amenities, and so forth. The report should also reflect any credits that the sellers gave the buyers for repairs—in other words, IOUs to be paid from the proceeds of the sale—which essentially function as reductions to the selling price. And the CMA should include comps currently on the market, waiting for offers, or final sales as we discussed in Chapter 1. They're another important factor in setting your list price.

Avoid Dual Agency

As a homeseller, you want your agent to represent your interests and help you achieve your goal: to sell your home quickly, for as much money as you can get. On the other side of the table is the buyer, who's hoping for the opposite: to get the property for as little as possible.

As you can imagine, it would be difficult for one agent to represent *both* of you, in what's called a dual agency. As adviser and Realtor® Nancy Atwood explains it, "The agent has a fiduciary duty to represent the interests of the seller—to get the seller the best deal possible. A dual agent then has the same duty to the buyer. These are opposite goals; the result is that the agent ends up really being nobody's agent, because it's impossible to represent both interests fully." And as adviser Mark Nash points out, "Some sellers think they'll save money by using a dual agent. But your potential cost savings can be undercut because you don't have an advocate on your side. You're better off with no agent than a dual agent."

Some agents prefer dual agency, because it means they don't have to split the commission with another agent. But you want to avoid it. If you're going to pay a full commission, you want someone who fully represents your interests. If an agent asks you to consent to a dual agency—such consent usually being required—flatly deny the request. Even better, ask any agent you're considering hiring, "Would you ever represent me in a dual agency?" That gets that preliminary issue out of the way.

Somewhat less onerous than the dual agency is a designated agency. In this situation, the buyer is represented by another agent in the same brokerage as your agent. Technically, this is a form of dual agency, because each agent works for the same broker. Unlike a dual agency, you get personal representation from a designated agent. But you must fully trust your agent to represent your interests and not divulge your bottom line to the buyer's agent.

If you're willing to participate in a designated agency, you might request a reduction in the commission, based on the fact that the brokerage will make twice as much as it otherwise would have on the deal.

TIP

Make sure the agent has actually visited most of the houses listed on your CMA. If not, the agent doesn't know much more than you do: the property's location and size, when it was listed and for how much, and when and if it sold and for how much. But an agent's personal knowledge of other properties—for example, that a house had an awkward floor plan or that its kitchen was recently remodeled—will be fundamental in determining how comparable those properties really are.

You'll also want to get information about the agent's sales history, so ask for a transaction report for the last year. This should contain the address, size, and number of rooms for each house the agent listed; the listing and sales dates; and the listing and sales prices. The object is to find out whether the agent sells homes regularly in your area; how long it takes the agent to sell properties, on average; whether there are any "dead spots" in the agent's history (if so, you can inquire as to why); and whether the agent sets realistic list prices. Though there's no way to get the entire picture just from the numbers, they give you a great starting point for asking more questions.

The other thing the agent should present is a marketing plan for your home. The presentation will be part background information—you'll probably learn about the agent's experience and history—but should be mostly focused on the agent's strategy for bringing your home to the attention of interested buyers. If it just seems like the agent is going to repeat a "tried and true" marketing plan, and the agent's sales numbers and times don't look exceptional, you can expect the same treatment everyone else gets, with the same mediocre results. "I spend a lot of time doing a 'pre-marketing plan,'" says adviser Mark Nash. "For example, I frequently get clients who are moving their elderly parents into care facilities and are selling the family home, which may need painting, updating, new landscaping, and so forth. I give them a list of things to do, and only after they've done them do we go in and take pictures and draw up marketing material that can highlight the positive changes."

> ⚠ **CAUTION**
>
> **Don't settle for a phone interview.** A prospective agent may promise to compile an adequate CMA just by talking to you on the phone. If so, it's a red flag to you: The agent isn't willing to put in the time to really make sure he or she understands how much your house is worth and how to position it competitively. Cross the agent off your list and choose someone more committed.

After doing the CMA, the agent should be able to suggest a listing price, or the range within which the listing price should fall. (This should be a fairly small range, however—hitting within the closest $50,000 or $100,000 mark hardly takes an expert's help.) Some agents, but by no means all, use their estimated list price as an opportunity to "reel you in," by giving you an unrealistically high figure, thus raising your hopes that the agent will sell your home for this inflated amount. This is called "buying" the listing. But as you well know, if the price is too high, it could easily have the opposite effect—your house will sit on the market, perhaps without attracting any interested buyers at all. At the very least, any offers that come in will be at a more realistic price, potentially causing serious disappointment. Make sure the agent is providing you with solid, recent data to back up any suggested list price.

Checklist: Items to Ask Agents For

At your meeting, the prospective agent should give you:

❑ the agent's CMA for your home

❑ information about the agent's sales history in the last year, and

❑ a comprehensive marketing plan/presentation.

Final Questions to Ask a Prospective Agent

In addition to presenting the information discussed above, your meetings with the remaining prospective agents (those whom you haven't already dropped from the running) provide an opportunity to ask questions. You're the boss here: You're looking for an agent who can really demonstrate an ability to get things done. We recommend spending as long as you need to get all these and any other questions answered:

 CAUTION
You should already have the answers to some of these questions.
However, we've included them anyway, to make sure you're covered.

- **How long have you been a real estate agent?** It's best to work with someone who has at least three years' experience in the residential real estate market where you live—even more is preferable, particularly because it means the agent has weathered other market downturns.

- **Are you a Realtor®?** Membership in the National Association of Realtors® (NAR) shows a continued interest in professional development, as well as a basic commitment to ethical behavior.

- **Do you have a broker's license?** To sell real estate, an agent needs only a salesperson's license. A broker's license is an extra step—again, evidence of the agent's commitment to professional development.

- **Do you have any professional designations or have you taken any specialized courses?** The NAR offers special designations for real estate agents, such as Certified Residential Specialist® (CRS®). Additionally, agents can take many different training classes to gain additional knowledge.

- **Do you work full-time?** It's imperative that your agent be readily available to respond to inquiries and show the property. While agents can't work around the clock, many routinely put in time on nights and weekends. Eliminate any agent who doesn't work full-time.

- **Would you ever represent me as a dual agent?** As already explained, you want an agent who represents your interests alone.

- **How many residential real estate transactions have you been a part of in the last year?** This should be a minimum of ten, to show that the agent is actively practicing.

- **In how many transactions did you represent the seller?** You want this to be at least half. Also ask how many of the houses sold.

- **Do you specialize in a certain type of property?** If so, make sure it's the kind of property you're selling: for example, a condominium, or an older home in a historic neighborhood.

- **Do you specialize in a certain geographic area?** Again, you'll want to make sure that if an agent has this type of specialty, it's in the area where you live. (But if you're buying in another area nearby and plan to use the same agent for both transactions, the agent probably won't be as experienced there.)

- **How will I reach you?** Are there days or times the agent is unavailable or will be on vacation? You want to know that it will be easy for you to call and check in and that the agent hasn't planned any lengthy hiatuses. Also make sure you're going to get personal service—that is, you're not going to be pushed off onto an aide.

- **How would you prepare my home for sale?** This is where the agent will describe any experience with staging and prepping a house for sale. While the agent may not want to give away "tricks of the trade" until you have a listing agreement, you're justified in asking for a general idea of what needs to be done, as well as for photos and ideas that explain what the agent has done to help other sellers.

- **Will you be providing me with a comparable market analysis?** The answer should be a definite "yes." You want some actual data to help price your home accurately.

- **What was the difference between the list price and selling price of homes you sold in the last year?** This is more of the hard data you'll need in evaluating whether the agent is realistic when pricing homes. Even if an agent tells you, "You can put your house on the market for $300,000," if similar listings by the agent at that price sold for only $250,000, you'll have a more realistic idea of what you're in for.

- **How long did the houses you've sold in the last six months take to sell?** If the agent's listings are languishing on the market for months at a time, that's what you can expect, too—either because your home won't be priced appropriately, or because the agent doesn't do enough to promote the sale. (However, an agent may have good explanations for aberrations—for example, an unreasonable seller who insisted on listing a property above market value or a house that needed major repairs and was therefore unappealing to most buyers.)

- **How many buyers and sellers are you currently representing?** Don't sign up with someone who's too busy to spend significant amounts of time with you. If the number sounds suspiciously high (say, above ten or so total clients at any given time) find out how the agent gets things done. You don't want to get pushed off to a less-experienced associate.

> **CAUTION**
>
> **There's no "right" number of clients.** As adviser Nancy Atwood explains, "Different agents can handle varying levels of work. While one agent may have her hands full with five clients, another may be able to take on ten and still provide excellent service." Use the agent's response to this question to find out how much time the agent spends taking care of each property and how available the agent will be to help you sell yours.

- **How exactly would you market my property?** Give the agent the opportunity to present you with a comprehensive marketing plan. You want to know that you're going to approach the process systematically. For specific marketing ideas, see Chapter 7.

- **Can you provide references?** Ask for at least three names of current or former clients who sold their homes within the last year. (You want people who sold their homes in similar market conditions.) Call and ask them how they liked working with the agent (and whether they'd do so again), what the agent's strengths and weaknesses are, and how long their homes were listed prior to sale.

A full list of these questions appears on the following page. You can keep this list in front of you when you meet with each prospective agent, taking notes as you go.

Checklist: Questions for Your Agent

❏ How long have you been a real estate agent?

❏ Are you a Realtor®?

❏ Do you have a broker's license?

❏ Do you have any professional designations or have you taken any specialized courses?

❏ Do you work full-time?

❏ Would you ever represent me as a dual agent?

❏ How many residential real estate transactions have you been a part of in the last year?

❏ In how many transactions did you represent the seller?

❏ Do you specialize in a certain type of property?

❏ Do you specialize in a certain geographic area?

❏ How will I reach you?

❏ How would you prepare my home for sale?

❏ Will you provide me with a comparable market analysis?

❏ What was the difference between the list price and selling price of homes you sold in the last six months?

❏ How long did the houses you've sold in the last six months take to sell?

❏ How many buyers and sellers are you currently representing?

❏ How exactly would you market my property?

❏ Can you provide at least three names of recent clients who sold their homes with you in the last year and who will serve as references?

Making It Official

Once you've found the agent you want to work with, you'll draw up a formal agreement. First, you may want to decide the commission you'll pay. Then you can talk over some of the other details.

Negotiating the Agent's Commission

How much an agent charges is typically a matter of local custom, but usually falls somewhere between 5% and 6% of the home's selling price. However, there's no set rule about this. (In fact, we've never heard a fully satisfactory answer as to why the amount of the payment should be locked to the selling price, as opposed to using some other factor like an hourly or task-based wage.)

Some real estate agents bristle when you try to negotiate a lower commission. They may begin to explain all the services they'll provide to you at the price they've set—the commission dictated by industry standard. Even if you're convinced the agent will provide good service, there are several situations in which asking for a lower commission nevertheless makes sense. For example:

- **You plan to do some of the work yourself.** If you're going to take on any part of the transaction that an agent would normally be expected to handle—creating your own website or showing the home to prospective purchasers, for example—you're justified in asking for a reduction in the commission.

- **The agent ends up selling to an unrepresented buyer or a buyer represented by another agent in the same brokerage.** For reasons we've explained, you don't want an agent who's selling to his or her own client to attempt to represent both of you. But if the agent isn't paying a commission to another agent, part of that savings should be passed off to you. Similarly, if the agent sells through another agent in the same brokerage, the brokerage can come out ahead by collecting fees from both agents. It's fair for you to request a share of that savings.

CAUTION

Don't agree to a reduced commission if the agent takes all. An agent may be willing to take a reduced commission if it won't be shared with an agent for the buyer—essentially, if the agent plans to find an unrepresented buyer without assistance. This is no bargain for you, because no other agent with a prospective buyer will have any incentive to show your home. You'll be depending solely on your agent to make a sale happen. A better approach is to agree to a higher commission if an outside agent is involved, but a lower commission if an unrepresented buyer happens to come along.

- **You plan to use the same agent to sell and buy.** If you're going to use the same agent to sell this house and purchase your next one, it's worth asking the agent to sell your house at a discount, knowing the agent will receive a commission on your purchase, too.

- **You feel market conditions are right.** When the real estate market is slow, agents have less work. That puts you in a better negotiating position, because agents can't be as picky or drive as hard a bargain. You might want to try and negotiate down the commission even for standard services. If one agent won't agree, another one might.

Of course, no agent is going to accept a deal if there's hardly any money to be made on it, and they'll have to get the broker's approval, too. On top of that, the agent will have to either find a buyer's agent who is willing to take a reduced commission or take the entire reduction alone. The second option is the best one from your point of view; reducing the buyer's agent's commission can mean fewer prospective buyers coming to check your place out.

CROSS-REFERENCE

Interested in hiring a discount agent? That option, as well as other options somewhere between hiring a full-service agent and selling entirely on your own, are discussed in the next chapter.

You may discuss negotiating the commission from the very beginning, when you first interview the agent. That way, an agent who really isn't willing to negotiate can let you know up front, making it easier for you to decide whether you want to work together.

On the other hand, you may tempt the agent even more if you bring up the commission later, when you're ready to sign a listing agreement. After all, the agent will be pleased to hear you say, "I'd like us to work together." Having already invested some time and effort, the agent may find it that much harder to turn down an offer that requires conceding only a little on the commissions front.

Your last opportunity to negotiate the commission will come when a buyer presents an offer, and this arguably gives you the most leverage in negotiating. If the offer is lower than you'd hoped for, you may let the agent know that you'd be willing to take the offer if the agent is willing to accept a lower commission. Agents who are motivated to close the deal may agree to this.

TIP

Make sure you know the commission split. Your agent should tell you how he or she will split the commission with the buyer's agent: 50/50 is most common. However, some sellers' agents keep a bigger share of the pie, and that reduces the incentive for buyers' agents to show your home. If you're paying the standard commission where you live, make sure the buyer's agent gets at least half—ask your agent if he or she doesn't volunteer the information or it doesn't appear in your listing contract.

Keep in mind that paying a full commission to a good agent is better than paying a reduced commission to a lousy one. You'll hopefully sell for more money thanks to a good agent's expertise, hard work, and savvy. This can more than make up for the hassle, expense, or delay of getting stuck listing with a dud.

Signing a Listing Agreement

Once you and your agent have agreed on the commission amount, you're going to sign a "listing agreement": a contract that says that the agent has the right to list your house. It's important to understand the terms of the agreement, because you'll be bound by them. And while a listing agreement is good for the agent, because it obligates you to work with the agent for at least a minimum amount of time, it also protects you, by explaining the agent's responsibilities and what you can do if he or she doesn't meet them.

After working out the issue of a commission (which will also be formalized in the agreement), you must decide what kind of relationship you'll have with your agent. Your primary options are:

- **Exclusive right to sell.** This will probably be your agent's first choice: It means that the agent has the exclusive right to sell your property for the duration of the agreement. Even if you find a buyer completely on your own, for instance the friend of a friend whom you run into at the grocery store, you'll still owe the agent a cut.

- **Exclusive agency.** This type of contract says that your agent is the only agent authorized to sell your house. But since you're not an agent, if you bring in the buyer yourself, you won't owe the agency anything. This may sound like a good plan, because if you can find someone to buy the place, the agent won't take a cut. On the other hand, it reduces the agent's incentive to put time and effort into marketing your house, because if you find a buyer first, all the agent's hard work will have been for nothing.

- **Open listing.** With an open listing, you agree to pay a commission to whichever real estate agent brings in a buyer. Good luck. You'd end up in nearly the same position as a seller who isn't using an agent at all, because it's extremely unlikely than any one agent is going to try to market your property. Agents don't want to waste their time, knowing that if someone else ultimately finds a willing buyer for your house, that lucky agent will snag the commission.

Most listing agents use standard forms, created by state or local Realtor® associations, to create the listing agreement. No surprise, these are generally written to protect the agent. So if you use one of these forms, read it very carefully. Make sure it looks out for your interests and accurately reflects what you talked over with your agent. Here are some of the most important terms such an agreement will cover:

- **Duration.** Your listing agreement will last for a set amount of time. From your perspective, a shorter listing agreement is better. If you don't like the agent's services, you can walk away and choose a different agent. Of course, from the agent's perspective, a longer listing agreement is preferable, because the agent is going to do a lot of work to get the house ready to sell, and won't want to risk losing a commission just as it's starting to garner some real interest. Adviser Joel G. Kinney says, "I recommend 90-day listing agreements to all my clients. A lot of agents want six months, but if the house isn't moving, you want the option of trying a different listing agent or taking it off the market without interfering with the agreement with your agent." Ninety days should also be enough time for the listing agent to effectively market the property and make the sale. If you're happy with the agent's services at the end of the listing period, you can always renew the agreement.

- **Safety or protection clause.** Even though the contract has an expiration date, it will probably also include a clause that protects the agent or broker after that date. This prevents you from trying to avoid paying an agent's commission by finding a buyer while you're represented by the agent, but waiting to conduct the sale until your listing agreement expires. You'll want an exception if you are ending the contract because you decide to change listing agents, however—if that agent sells quickly and your clause entitles the first agent to a cut, you could owe two commissions.

> **CAUTION**
>
> **You may owe a commission on an offer you turn down!** Most standard listing agreements say that the listing agent earns payment upon bringing in a buyer with an "acceptable" offer. If you receive a full-price offer but decide you're not going to sell (without having a legitimate reason), your listing agreement may obligate you to pay the commission.

- **Duties.** The agreement may lay out the activities the agent is authorized to conduct on your behalf. Read through the list carefully, making sure you understand everything. If there are specific duties you want to require of the agent—for example, listing the property on the MLS, posting a yard sign, or creating a listing sheet—specify those as well.

- **Representations.** The agreement may also require you to verify certain facts—for instance, that you're in a legal position to sell the property and that to your knowledge no one else has an ownership interest in it.

- **Dispute resolution.** The agreement will probably specify how you will handle disputes that you can't work out informally, such as through mediation or binding arbitration.

Most standard contracts will include these issues. Don't sign without reading carefully, however—and don't be afraid to ask for any changes or amendments. Agents may resist changing their standard agreements, having used them many times in the past without incident. Nevertheless, if you're uncomfortable with something, there's no reason it can't be changed. Small changes can be written right on the contract (make sure you get a copy), and large changes can be added on separate addendums and referred to in the contract itself (there's usually a space for additional terms; here you can refer to the addendum). ●

Save on Commissions: Sell It Yourself

Meet Your Adviser

George Devine, licensed real estate broker, author, and educator in the real estate field

. . . .

What he does: He founded and owns George Devine, Realtor®, a family residential brokerage in San Francisco, which has been assisting sellers and buyers for over 30 years (see www.georgedevinerealtor.com). Devine also teaches real estate at the School of Business and Management at the University of San Francisco, where he was named Outstanding Adjunct Professor in 1991. And, he's the author of *For Sale by Owner in California* and co-author of *How to Buy a House in California* (both published by Nolo).

Favorite money-saving strategy in tough times: "Actually, it's not just for tough times, but it's a good reminder for sellers who are looking to buy another home. Don't just consider the price of the house in isolation. Also calculate how much it costs you to get between home and work—what I call the 'home-work factor.' Let's suppose you're looking at houses in two nearby towns, one of which ('X town'), is close to your office, the other of which ('Y town') is many miles farther away. The prospective house in Y town is much cheaper, and will run you $300 a month less in mortgage interest, so you're seriously tempted. But don't forget to calculate the added commuting costs to get from X town to your office, such as public transit costs or more likely gas, oil, car maintenance, and the occasional cost of picking up takeout on the way home because you're too frazzled to make dinner—none of which are tax deductible. Meanwhile, the mortgage interest you'd pay for the house in X town is tax deductible from ordinary income. That can be a big piece of change!"

Likes best about his work:	"I get to meet interesting people and participate in key moments in their lives. I learn something new from each transaction. There's not one that I come away from saying 'ho hum.'"
Strangest thing he's seen sellers do:	"I've seen a few strange things over the years—sellers opening the door in their underwear, bursting into obscenities at the closing because something unexpected came up, or trying to sell a house without cleaning up after the incontinent cats."
Top tip for homesellers:	"Invest the money in staging your house. It's making a bigger difference now than ever before, because an unstaged home suggests that the owners aren't serious about doing business. I brought one buyer to a house in the Potrero Hill neighborhood in San Francisco that had an awkwardly built stairway, and he slipped and practically broke his leg—but still loved the home because it was so beautifully staged."

As we discussed in the last chapter, your biggest homeselling expense will probably be the fee you pay to your real estate agent: on average, 5% to 6% of the selling price. Even though it's split with the buyer's agent, you, as the seller, pay the entire thing. At a time when you're trying to save money, the idea of spending thousands of dollars on this one expense, potentially wiping out some or all of your equity—or in the worst case, requiring you to dig into your own pocket—can be frustrating.

To save money, you may consider selling your home yourself, without the help of a real estate professional. This is sometimes called "for sale by owner" or FSBO (pronounced "fizz-bo"). It's a controversial option within the real estate industry, with some arguing that inexperienced sellers often fail to bring in as high a price as an experienced real estate agent could, thus undercutting their commission savings; and others maintaining that with commissions so high, even a seller who makes a few mistakes will come out ahead. This chapter will explore these and other issues regarding selling on your own. We'll cover:

- the advantages and disadvantages of going FSBO
- how much you'll save, and whether to pay a buyer's agent
- how to market and advertise your FSBO, and
- alternatives to selling FSBO.

FSBO—The Way to Go?

Going FSBO offers some distinct advantages, including:

- **Reduced cost.** Probably the number one reason people sell on their own is to save the commission they'd otherwise pay.
- **More control.** As a FSBO seller, you'll have exclusive control over the listing price, form of advertising, when and how to show the house, negotiating the contract, and more.
- **Pricing competitively.** If you're not paying a commission, you may be able to reduce your house's asking price, essentially "sharing" your savings with the buyer. This should bring in more prospective buyers. (But

before you figure out how low to go, decide whether you plan to pay a commission to the buyer's agent, as discussed below.)

What Do the Stats Show About FSBO Sellers Saving Money?

Ask any real estate agent and you're bound to hear that going FSBO is a near-fatal mistake. According to the National Association of Realtors®, the average price of a house sold by owner in 2007 was $187,200, while the average sale price for an agent-sold home was $247,000. This suggests that homes sell for more when sold by an agent.

On the other side of the table, however, a 2008 study by *Consumer Reports* found that FSBO sellers get more for their homes—around $5,000 more, on average. And in the middle, a 2007 study out of Stanford University found that using a broker didn't affect the average selling price of homes on its campus (though the houses sold a little faster when a broker was involved). So who's right?

It's hard to say—but there's no reason to spend a lot of time worrying about it. If you follow the advice in this book, you'll be able to handle some of the primary tasks normally carried out by agents. You'll set a realistic price for your home and learn how to aggressively market it, show it, and negotiate a sale. As adviser George Devine puts it, "If you can follow some of the programs that help you do your own taxes, you can do this."

- **Knowledge.** No one knows your house and neighborhood better than you do. You're in the best position to impart that knowledge to a potential buyer.

There are disadvantages to selling FSBO, however. These include:

- **Lack of experience.** You won't have the experience a real estate professional will have with the sales process in general and with sales trends in your geographic area. That may mean that you have to rely on other professionals and educate yourself on some topics.

CAUTION

Don't let your lack of experience cost you. "I've seen FSBO sellers really alienate buyers, and that can risk deals," says Realtor® and adviser Mark Nash. "For example, FSBO sellers who don't understand the home inspection process sometimes balk at perfectly reasonable requests by the buyers to make basic repairs in the $500 range. An agent would tell a seller with a good offer not to let something so minor jeopardize the deal. But unless the seller understands the risks and sees that making the repairs is the smartest move, they risk angering the buyer and potentially losing the deal."

- **Time and effort.** Selling on your own is a big time commitment. You'll have to do all the tasks a real estate agent would have handled. (For a review of these tasks, take a look back at Chapter 4.) Not only will you have to learn how to price and market your property, you'll have to show it to every interested buyer. When you do receive an offer, you'll have to evaluate it and handle all the paperwork associated with it. On the other hand, as adviser George Devine notes, "If you're one of the many victims of a layoff, you probably have more time than money at your disposal— and will likely find, if you compare the number of hours you'll spend selling FSBO to the amount you'll save on the commission, that it's time profitably spent."

- **Difficulty advertising.** Many buyers today look for homes on the Internet. The most common way for buyers to access the fullest range of home choices is on the local Multiple Listing Service (MLS). FSBO sellers can get their homes listed on the MLS (we'll explain how below), but it's often expensive. In fact, FSBO sellers will have to do all their own advertising in general, including yard signs, open houses, and listing sheets. It can also be harder to distribute this material when not working with an agent, who is in constant contact with potential buyers and other agents.

- **Additional costs.** Even though you'll pay a lot less when you sell FSBO, you may not save the entire 5% to 6% commission. You'll have to fork out cash for advertising, potentially pay a commission to the buyer's agent (as discussed below), and perhaps hire an attorney to review your contract, even if that's not required where you live. In short, some of your savings may be offset by other costs.

Before deciding you're ready to go FSBO, carefully weigh these pros and cons, and honestly consider whether you have the time, skill, knowledge, and perhaps most importantly, desire to get the job done—or to learn how to do it. You should be highly motivated if you're selling FSBO, because you're your own salesperson. Your enthusiasm and perseverance will translate directly into how well you're able to generate interest in the property, thereby increasing the chances it will sell. Still interested? Keep reading.

A Cooperating Commission for the Buyer's Agent?

Saving 5% to 6% sounds good, but would selling FSBO still be worthwhile if you saved only half that amount? You'll probably be faced with that question, for the simple reason that any prospective buyers who are using their own agent will need to find a way to pay that agent. And they're probably hoping you'll provide that payment—in real estate terms, you'll "cooperate."

You may think that paying a buyer's agent's commission defeats the purpose of selling FSBO in the first place—here you are trying to save money, only to pay an agent who isn't even there to serve your needs. And if you're selling to someone you know, paying an agent a significant commission may seem particularly nonsensical, since one of the agent's primary tasks—matching the buyer to the seller—has already been taken care of.

Don't, however, automatically write off paying a cooperating commission. If you haven't yet found a buyer, a large part of marketing your property will involve getting the word out that it's for sale. Though the Internet is a fabulous tool for this, agents still play a significant role in matching buyers to sellers. And when agents know they won't get a commission from you, they're not motivated to show your listing to their prospective clients. They may discourage clients from looking at the place, or tell them horror stories of the difficulties of working directly with FSBO sellers who don't understand real estate customs and procedures. Letting agents know that you'll pay the cooperating commission keeps them motivated to show your home.

Also, involving a real estate agent means you won't be responsible for educating the buyer. While you'll need to do your own legwork to make the transaction successful, on the other side of the table you'll have a professional who knows how the process works and can provide the buyer with standard offer forms and advice.

But don't assume paying the commission means the buyer's agent will educate *you*. It isn't the buyer's agent's responsibility to handle tasks your agent normally would. In fact, that's not what you want. As Nancy Atwood points out, "A buyer's agent has a fiduciary duty to represent the buyer's interests." If you're not willing to hire an agent of your own, Atwood advises, "The first thing you should do is hire a lawyer."

To save everyone time, consider deciding whether you'll pay a cooperating commission ahead of time. If you announce your willingness up front, you won't have to deal with as many phone calls from agents, and you can rest assured that agents will be more motivated to show your house to clients.

TIP

Don't pay twice. If you both lower your listing price to account for the full 5% to 6% commission *and* pay a buyers' agent, you'll lose out. If you're trying to attract buyers with a below-market list price, better to lower it by one or two percentage points and leave room to both pay a buyer's agent and compensate yourself for the efforts of selling FSBO.

Doing Your Own Marketing and Advertising

One of the biggest challenges to selling your property yourself is making sure that buyers know it's for sale. The Internet has made this much easier. In years prior, real estate agents jealously guarded information about homes for sale that today is just a few mouse clicks away.

In Chapter 7, we'll cover some of the more general marketing strategies anyone can use to sell their home. Here, we'll focus in on a few key tricks you'll need to know as a FSBO seller.

Marketing Online

According to the National Association of Realtors®, in 2006, 84% of prospective homebuyers looked for properties online. And the numbers are no doubt rising, as younger, Internet-savvy buyers enter the market. It stands to reason that you'll be able to expose your house to many of these buyers if you advertise it on the right websites.

Listing on the MLS

Most real estate agents list homes for sale on the Multiple Listing Service (MLS). Each MLS is a localized database of homes for sale in that area. While it used to be that only real estate agents could list homes for sale on the MLS or use it to access information about available homes, much of the information is now readily accessible by consumers. Many MLS systems feed information to other databases; for example, to realtor.com (the website for the National Association of Realtors®), msn.com, and local newspaper or individual real estate agents' websites.

Several online FSBO websites (discussed further below) will list your home on the MLS for a flat fee, usually a few hundred dollars. You might also be able to find an agent willing to list your property for a small fee. (Currently, the website www.iggyshouse.com will list your house on the MLS at no cost. However, you must first list the property on the company's website, and you may be contacted about using the company's counterpart, BuySide Realty, to purchase your next home.)

In Chapter 7, we'll explain more about what specific pieces of information you should highlight in your MLS listing. As a FSBO seller, however, you should add to that list a mention of whether you're willing to pay a cooperating commission—the buyer's agent's commission discussed above—and if so, how much you'll pay.

FSBO Websites

The MLS isn't the only place buyers look for homes online. Several Web services offer advertising opportunities geared specifically to FSBO properties. Some of the more popular include forsalebyowner.com and fsbo.com. On these and other sites, you can pay a relatively modest fee (beginning at less than $100) to list your home on that particular site and often slightly higher fees (up to around $1,000) for additional services like a yard sign, a virtual tour, listing on the MLS, and color brochures or flyers.

Creating Your Own Website or Blog

You can create Web exposure for your home on your own, too. One easy way is to create a website or blog. It's easy to purchase a domain name at websites like godaddy.com or domain.com. These companies will also provide services to help you set up your website. Many sellers purchase their home's address as a domain name—for example, www.123mainstreet.com—and use this URL on promotional materials and yard signs.

Creating a blog is also easy and can be free. Unlike a website, blogs are created mostly to convey text or static information—pictures instead of virtual tours, for example—but can be just as effective. Go to a publishing tool like blogger.com or wordpress.com; both will walk you through the steps to create the blog and allow you to include both pictures and text.

As far as content, it's best to make sure your blog or website contains a lot of the same information as on your listing sheet (discussed further below). However, you have the opportunity to include more here. Pictures are probably the most important: Buyers are on the Internet to see homes they're interested in purchasing and to avoid wasting their time visiting homes that don't match their wishes. Take pictures on a sunny day when the house is clean and well staged (as described in Chapter 3). Include a diversity of shots, such the main living areas, functional outdoor areas, the master bedroom, perhaps one other bedroom, and the best of your bathrooms.

TIP

Use social networking sites to promote your house. If you network with friends on sites like Facebook (www.facebook.com) or MySpace (www.myspace.com), don't forget to mention your homeselling plans and link to your house's Website or blog.

Should You Take Out a Classified Ad?

The traditional way to generate interest in a FSBO was to put a classified ad in your local newspaper. But now, it's probably not worth the effort or the cost. Buyers able to take full virtual tours online are less interested in 20-word descriptions full of cryptic abbreviations.

If you can't afford to get on the MLS, you might try an online classified ad either through your local newspaper (a small neighborhood paper may be cheaper and more effective than one serving your whole city) or on Craigslist (craigslist.org). If you do take out an ad in the paper, we suggest you include the property's Web address in the listing, so that buyers can look for themselves.

Posting Signs

One good, old-fashioned way to get the word out that your house is for sale is to post a sign in your front yard. While picking up a simple "For Sale" sign at your local hardware store is probably the cheapest option (short of scrawling the words on a piece of cardboard), it's also likely to be the least effective. The information you write on the sign, such as your contact information or the list price, will be too small for anyone driving by to read. And a small sign doesn't look very professional, either.

Instead, have a sturdy, professional sign made that you can put close to the road, allowing anyone driving or walking by to see it clearly. The sign should include a phone number where prospective buyers can reach you. You may even consider designating a phone line to provide prerecorded information about the house to interested buyers.

CAUTION

Don't be surprised by a knock on the door. Some interested buyers think that selling FSBO means you're willing to take personal inquiries at any time. If someone walking by knocks, try to schedule a time for a showing.

If you use the services of an online FSBO website, it may offer packages that include a yard sign. If so, you'll want to know whether the sign comes with any "riders"—those extra templates that hang off the primary sign and can convey extra information, such as "Open Sunday 1-4." You also want to know whether you'll get a flyer box—that's the small box, often mounted on the sign post, that provides flyers to interested parties. If your sign will have a flyer box, keep it well stocked—we'll explain what to put on the flyer in the next section.

Creating a Listing Sheet

A flyer or "listing sheet" can be a useful and multifunctional marketing tool. You can not only put it out with your yard sign, but also distribute it at open houses or when you give tours or send it around to neighbors (who might spread the word to their friends).

Your goal with a listing sheet is twofold: to give the buyer a little information about the place and to make it attractive and memorable so the prospective buyer will either visit it or remember it after a visit. But what you don't want to do is overwhelm readers with information or give away so much that the prospective buyer no longer feels the need to check things out personally. To make your flyer stand out:

- **Use a header.** In font larger than the rest of the text, catch the buyer's eye with a descriptive and intriguing heading, such as "Picture-Perfect Starter in Desirable Heritage Park."

- **Include photos.** You'll need at least a picture of the home's exterior. If you can add a flattering, perhaps smaller, indoor shot or two, even better.

- **Keep it short.** Describe the basics—the number of bedrooms, bathrooms, square feet, when the house was built, and so forth. You might use bullet points to convey this information, but don't drone on and on—the flyer will look busy, and you won't leave any mystery.

- **Be descriptive.** Mention the home's best features, such as "refinished hardwood floors throughout and kitchen fully remodeled in 2006." Focus on elements that will capture a buyer's interest, such as the environmentally friendly solar panels and tankless water heater, the luxurious master suite, or the fully landscaped backyard paradise.

- **Make it readable.** Don't try to jam too much text into too small a space, like with eight-point font. If it's too small, buyers won't be able to read it and will lose interest.

- **Highlight your contact information.** Make it easy for a prospective buyer to reach you. Don't put your home phone number on the sheet if you really only use your cell phone. On the other hand, don't put your cell phone number down if you're not willing to take calls pretty much any time of day. For buyers who are curious but maybe not ready to talk to you, include your Web address or blog.

Open Houses

If you were to hire an agent, he or she would likely conduct open houses and politely ask you to clear out of the house for the day. There's a good reason for your absence. It's hard to hear criticisms about the color of your bedroom walls or the kitchen remodel you so lovingly slaved over. And unlike you, an agent is trained not to seem too eager (which can seem desperate or invasive) when a prospective buyer shows interest.

When selling your house FSBO, however, you won't have an agent to act as a buffer. That means you'll have to temper any natural defensive or stalking mechanisms when doing your open houses.

Should you even do open houses at all? While they're of questionable value when you hire an agent (some agents use them as an opportunity to fish for new clients, rather than to focus on selling your house), when you're on your own, they can be important for creating publicity that you might not otherwise get. After all, local agents may not even know your property is for sale, or in the worst case, may try to discourage prospective buyers from looking at it, especially if you don't offer to pay the cooperating commission.

Responding to Agent Inquiries

As a FSBO seller, you'll probably be approached by at least one real estate agent looking to help take the property off your hands by listing it with him or her. If so, you needn't necessarily dismiss the offer out of hand. If you're willing to pay a cooperating commission if the agent brings you a buyer, point that out.

If the agent tries to convince you that he or she will be able to help you make a deal, ask for specifics on how these marketing efforts will work better than your own. Don't be afraid to stick to your guns—if you change your mind later, you'll have no trouble finding an agent to work with (using the strategies we discussed in the last chapter to find a great agent).

If an agent claims to have an interested buyer, be receptive but cautious. Some agents don't have any specific buyer or may have several they'd show your property to, but are really just looking for another way to get you to list your property with them. Invite the agent to bring the buyer on a home tour, but don't waste a lot of time on the phone discussing the particulars. And keep in mind—anything you disclose to the agent is likely to get back to the prospective buyer or buyers.

So get ready to conduct your own open house and maybe more than one. Your job at an open house is to be a salesperson—to acquaint prospective buyers with your home's many amenities, without laying it on so thick they feel overwhelmed and run out the door. Here are some tips for doing this best:

- **Set your open house for a convenient time.** Open houses traditionally occur on weekends, and last for at least a couple hours. One way to increase traffic is to choose another convenient time—perhaps a weekday evening—and maybe offer some snacks, too. If you're used to seeing open houses at certain times in the neighborhood—for example, 1-4 on a Sunday—you may also increase traffic just by starting a little earlier and running a little later (such as 12-5).

- **Set out several signs.** In addition to your regular yard sign, you may want to purchase one or more "directional" signs that tell prospective buyers where to go. You can place these at busy intersections near your place.

- **Welcome looky-lous.** You're sure to get neighbors who are just curious about what's for sale in the neighborhood and at what price. Instead of dismissing or being suspicious of such neighbors, welcome them in. You never know who they know—perhaps they'll tell others who are looking to buy.

- **Ask visitors to sign in.** This serves more than one purpose. First, it protects you—if you're going to open your home, you have a right to know who's in it. But it also gives you an opportunity to follow up. For example, you can call someone who seemed interested, ask whether they've had an opportunity to think about it, and offer to show them the place again.

- **Provide marketing material.** Make sure you've got plenty of copies of your listing sheet or other marketing material ready to hand out, so interested buyers can walk away with something.

- **Show visitors around.** This not only allows you to highlight your home's lovely features, it protects you. Occasionally, open houses are visited by people who have no interest in buying homes, but are instead planning to scope them out and help themselves to things they find. You can protect yourself by carefully storing your valuables and medicines, and keeping an eye on who's in the place. Watch out for the old trick of one person engaging you in an intense conversation while the other one roams your house alone. (It may take more than one person to deal with multiple visitors, so enlist the help of a partner or friend, if necessary.)

- **Get the kids and pets out.** You're sure to be distracted if you have little ones—or furry ones—running around. And both take away from a buyer's ability to see themselves living in the home.

- **Dress appropriately.** You're not having friends over for a weekend barbeque. This is a professional transaction, so dress the part—a full suit probably isn't necessary, but business-casual attire shows you're to be taken seriously.

- **Make your home look great.** Follow the advice in Chapters 2 and 3 to ensure the property is in good shape before you throw open your doors.

Showing Your House

In addition to open houses, you'll be responsible for showing your house to interested buyers by appointment—sometimes more than once. Making sure the house is in tip-top shape for each viewing takes enough time as it is, but it's only the beginning if you're a FSBO seller.

The problem with showing your house yourself is that you don't want to come off too strong. While you're motivated to sell the place, you don't want the prospective buyer to feel like there's a salesperson crawling down his or her throat, trying to force a sale.

At the same time, you don't want to reveal too much. For example, if a prospective buyer asks you why you're moving, don't launch into a discussion about the great new job you're starting in a week, in a city across the country. You don't want to divulge any clues about how desperate you are to sell or how low a price you'd be willing to accept.

Instead, treat the visit like an individual open house—an opportunity to show the place off to someone you hope, but don't assume, is interested in buying the place. As with an open house, plan to walk through together. You can offer general information about each room, such as "This is the only bedroom on this floor; the floors were refinished two years ago," but you shouldn't provide an exhaustive list of every detail about the room and certainly not information about the occupants—that's the last thing the buyer wants to hear. Allow the buyer some quiet time to look without listening to you.

While you allow buyers to enter a room and look around, don't follow right on their heels. Instead, hang back around the doorway. Make sure they know you're available to answer any questions (and make sure you know the answers to the most basic ones, like when remodeling projects were completed).

When prospective buyers are ready to leave, remind them how to contact you with any questions. Also double check that you have their contact information. You may want to follow up in a few days, just to see if they have any additional questions.

Receiving an Offer and Negotiating a FSBO Deal

After all your hard work, you'll be thrilled if and when you finally get an offer. But don't celebrate just yet. Many real estate offers—especially in a down market, when buyers are wondering whether it wouldn't be better to wait for even lower prices—never make it to sales. And even if they do, there are lots of other steps first.

To understand the terms of any offer you'll receive and how to negotiate the sale, take a peek at Chapter 10. It covers these issues in detail. Here, we're going to talk about two key issues unique to FSBO offers: how to handle negotiations in person and how to get the help you need to close the deal.

> **TIP**
>
> **Look especially hard at the buyer's finances.** It doesn't do you much good to accept an offer and negotiate a deal only to find out that the buyer can't get a mortgage to buy the place. As a FSBO seller, one of your most important tasks when reviewing an offer—particularly if the buyer is unrepresented—is to examine the buyer's financial situation. We'll give details on how to do that in Chapter 10.

Negotiating With the Buyer

Negotiating successfully is a skill and one of the reasons many people choose an agent in the first place. You and the buyer have two very different objectives: You want to sell the house for as much as you can, and the buyer wants to buy it for as little as possible. You can take a hard-line approach: "I won't take a penny less than my asking price!" or "I need at least 60 days to complete this sale and move out!" But it's less likely to keep the buyer's interest.

In most states, reaching an agreement doesn't normally involve sitting down and hashing things out with a buyer, however. That's because the real estate industry has developed a more formalized means of negotiation, in which the seller and the buyer, usually through their agents, exchange written offers and counteroffers, perhaps with a formal, in-person meeting at the very beginning. Exactly how that's done is a matter of local custom and whether the buyer is represented by a real estate agent. You don't literally have to send or deliver original documents via U.S. mail—it's typical to exchange faxes or email attachments and then later follow up with the original.

On the other hand, if you find it easier, there's nothing to stop you and the buyer from sitting down at a table together and going over the details until you've reached a solid agreement. How comfortable you feel with the buyer may also play into this decision. If you end up selling to a good friend of the neighbor who you've met at social events, it may be easier and more comfortable to get together—even in the house—to work out the deal. Just make sure you don't get so lulled into a sense of comfort and complacency that you start making concessions you wouldn't otherwise. And if you expect multiple offers, you might set a date and time by which you must receive them.

The last step in your negotiations should be for both of you to sign the purchase contract. No matter who goes first, you don't have a contract until both of you have signed. See Chapter 10 for an analysis of what goes into the purchase contract, including which terms are or aren't worth negotiating hard over.

It's a good idea to review a blank offer, contract, disclosures, and other forms—if you're using a standard set—before you begin any negotiations, says adviser Mark Nash. "You won't have someone there representing your interests, so you need to hit the ground running." Both Nash and adviser Nancy Atwood agree that if you're going to represent yourself, it's vital that you hire an attorney to represent you in the transaction. "Given the value of what's at stake—a house—it's worth the several hundred dollars in lawyer's fees," points out Nash. In addition to helping you understand the standard forms, your attorney can tell you of any special contract requirements in your state, plus review the completed agreement with you. In some states, a title officer may be able to provide you with copies of standard documents—just don't expect much else, as it's not the title officer's job to educate or represent you.

Closing the Deal

Your purchase contract is an important legal document, signifying that neither of you can back out of the sale without a valid reason. But that doesn't seal the deal—there's more work to be done to finalize everything.

For one, the document itself will doubtless contain several valid reasons (called contingencies) that protect either you or the buyer, by allowing either of you to cancel the deal if certain criteria aren't met. For example, if your contract has an inspection contingency, the buyer can conduct an inspection and condition the sale on approving the results.

And that's just the beginning. We'll discuss more of this in Chapter 10, but the bottom line is that the deal isn't over until weeks after the purchase contract is signed, when the sale has formally closed and the deed has been recorded. Although the buyer will be doing a lot of the work—coordinating inspections, lining up financing, and so forth—you'll want to make sure he or she is meeting any deadlines outlined in your agreement.

And you may have your own requirements to meet, for example, obtaining a clearance letter from your homeowners' association saying that you don't owe any outstanding fees or dues. Fortunately, you won't need to handle all of this alone—you'll hire a neutral third party, either an escrow or title agent (their name and role depends on what state you live in) to organize and orchestrate many of the details and make sure you and the buyer both do what you're supposed to do to make the transaction happen.

Also, as we explained above, because you may be responsible for some steps with serious legal consequences—for example, preparing the deed or making sure title is clear—you may want an attorney to ensure you handle everything correctly. (Hiring one to review your work, when possible, will be significantly cheaper than hiring one to do the work from scratch.) If you're in a state where title companies handle escrow, the title agent may do some of this for you.

Almost FSBO: Discount Agents and Other Alternatives

The world of FSBO isn't for everyone—but there are ways to dip your toes in the water without getting soaked. While real estate agents have a standard set of services for which they usually charge a standard price (5% to 6%), there's no hard and fast rule that says it must be this way. Here are a few alternatives:

- **Negotiate a lower commission.** Particularly in slow markets, when they're having a hard time making sales, agents may be willing to work for less. You'll usually find independent brokers and new agents are most amenable to this, and you shouldn't expect to knock more than 1% to 2% off the amount (your agent will still have to pay the cooperating commission to the buyer's broker and will insist on making something on the deal). You may also find a broker willing to charge less than full commission if there's no cooperating agent involved—that is, if they can find a buyer themselves.

- **Find a discount agent.** A discount agent will cost less than a full-service agent, but also provide fewer services. For example, a discount agent might take care of marketing the property, but leave it up to you to show it to prospective purchasers.

- **Pay for certain services.** You may be able to find an agent who will only do—and charge you for—certain services. Most commonly, sellers pay agents just to list their property on the MLS. But there's no reason you can't hire an agent for the limited purpose of negotiating an agreement, reviewing your contract, or showing your home, for example.

We could list other creative strategies we've heard of—hiring agents by the hour, paying an agent a flat rate instead of a commission—but finding an agent to agree to these strategies can be difficult. Still, it doesn't hurt to ask: The worst an agent can do is say no. Just keep in mind that finding a high-quality agent (we'll discuss how in the next chapter) is more important than finding an inexpensive one.

A final option is to try a more limited FSBO on your own, before listing the property with an agent. This will work well only if you are not in a hurry to sell, however. You can let friends, family, and colleagues know that you're interested in selling your home and are planning on listing with an agent soon. However, you can explain that you're willing to sell it for a little less than the price you planned to list at, if you and the buyer don't have to pay real estate commissions. You may even offer a small cash incentive to those who help you sell (discussed in Chapter 6). ●

Making It Better Than the Rest: Buyer Incentives

Meet Your Adviser

Asheesh Advani, founder of Virgin Money, USA, based in Waltham, Massachusetts, (see www.virginmoneyus.com) and an expert in alternative forms of home financing

What he does: With a background in finance and development economics, including a stint at the World Bank, Asheesh came to realize the enormous demand for loans that everyday people could access. To fill that gap, he founded CircleLending, Inc., in 2001, to facilitate interpersonal loans. Its rapid growth attracted the attention of Richard Branson's Virgin Group. As Virgin Money USA, the company has managed over $300 million in "person-to-person" loans and mortgages (including seller financings) every year.

Favorite money-saving strategy in tough times: "We save money by reducing travel costs by taking holidays closer to home. My wife (who serves as the family's CFO) and I are perennial globe trotters, having spent time working and studying on three continents since college. To save money in tough times, we bundle the kids in the car and drive around the country rather than take holiday flights abroad."

Likes best about his work: "Taking on challenges! It has been exhilarating to build the company from scratch, first as CircleLending then again as Virgin Money USA. CircleLending launched during the recession in 2001 and Virgin Money has had to persevere through the recession that started in 2008. It has been a joy to watch our ideas take shape as a company during these challenging times. And we're continually brainstorming—it's great working with people who have more ideas than we can ever hope to bring to life. Also, we feel like our product helps both home buyers and sellers, bringing about home sales that might never have happened otherwise."

Strangest thing he's seen sellers do: "Buyers hate it when sellers reveal problems with the home just before the closing. Yet, I have seen many closings delayed or cancelled because nervous sellers hide the bad news about a property until just before the closing—which is also when the buyer is most nervous about signing on the dotted line."

• •

Top tip for homesellers: "Interview multiple Realtors® before selecting the one that's right for you. Don't hire the first one referred to you by a friend. Don't hire the one that says that your home is worth more than it really is."

n a crowded market, when there are a lot more houses available than buyers wanting them, even a well-priced, well-staged home can get lost in the shuffle. And if you do find a buyer who likes the look of your house, you may need to offer some added incentives—most likely financial—to convince the buyer to choose your house over the competition. If you're not willing to offer a great deal, there's probably another seller out there who is.

In this chapter, we'll cover ways you can make your deal stand out from the rest, including by offering:

- seller financing for all or part of the loan
- payment of some of the purchase costs
- an option to lease the property now and buy later, and
- financial incentives to all the agents in the transaction.

These incentives can be either advertised from the start, negotiated with individual buyers, or added into the mix if your house isn't selling as quickly as anticipated.

Helping the Buyer With the Loan: Seller Financing

In the typical house sale, the buyer makes an offer and gets a mortgage from a bank or other financial institution. But there's no rule that says it has to happen this way. In fact, one attractive incentive you can offer is to act as the lender yourself. You won't literally hand cash to the buyer—instead, you'll extend credit to the buyer at the closing. In return, you'll get a deed of trust or a mortgage, which means if the buyer doesn't pay you back, you can foreclose on the property.

For as long as you're the lender, the buyer will make regular monthly payments to you. These payments will likely comprise both interest and principal, so you'll be earning money. But of course, you'll have walked away with less cash at closing, so this option works best if you own your house outright, have a lot of equity built up in it, or for some other reason don't need all the cash from the sale immediately.

Buyers who won't qualify for traditional financing on the terms they want are drawn to seller financing. They're hoping you'll be more flexible, or even generous, when it comes to deciding whether to loan money, what interest rate to charge, and how much to lend.

Another possible option to offer buyers who can't finance their entire purchase with a traditional lender is to fund a smaller, second mortgage. For example, a buyer who only has 10% to put down and can find a bank that will lend 80% of the purchase price might come to you for the 10% difference.

Seller-financed loans are frequently short term—say, three to five years—with a balloon payment due at the end. This allows the buyer some time to get financially stable, then find a traditional lender when his or her financial picture looks a little better. Hopefully, the buyer's income or credit will go up, interest rates will go down, the buyer will accrue some serious equity, or a combination of these factors will occur.

Advantages of Seller Financing

Seller financing isn't just good for the buyer. It provides you with advantages, too. These include:

- **Widening the scope of able buyers.** As mentioned, seller financing may be important to certain buyers who aren't able to obtain traditional financing. In a slow market, this can help you get your property sold.

- **Income.** You'll receive regular monthly cash, in the form of interest the buyer will pay on the loan, plus a portion of the principal the buyer is repaying bit by bit. (Of course, this assumes the buyer is responsible enough to pay—we'll get to that in a moment.)

- **Tax deferral.** If you have a lot of equity and expect to owe high capital gains taxes (most likely because you've owned the property for a long time, and it has appreciated significantly), you can spread out those taxes over the course of several years, as you receive the payments.

> ⓘ **CAUTION**
>
> **If you're counting on tax deferral, you may be in trouble if the buyer suddenly pays off the entire loan.** If that's a potential issue, you can include a prepayment penalty in your loan contract (but check your state's laws to see whether it sets a maximum on the amount allowed). Alternatively, you may want to write the loan terms to be so attractive that the buyer will never want to switch to a traditional lender. We'll explain more about how to do that below.

Another Seller Alternative: Wraparound Financing

There's an alternative some sellers use to provide financing, called a "wraparound." With a wraparound, you keep your original mortgage, then collect payments from the buyer. If you have a below-market interest rate, you can make money this way, by charging the buyer a higher interest rate and pocketing the difference.

But a wraparound is risky. First off, most conventional lenders won't allow it. If you don't disclose your arrangement to your lender and it's later discovered, you may find the lender immediately "calling" your loan—meaning you'll be forced to repay it in full, right away.

Second, if you offer a wraparound without securing a mortgage interest in the property (you'll have to, if you don't want the lender to know about it), and the buyer doesn't pay you, you don't have a recordable interest. That is, you can't foreclose on the property, even while you're stuck with the payment. For these reasons, a recorded mortgage is far preferable to a wraparound.

Disadvantages of Seller Financing

Probably the biggest disadvantage of seller financing is that if the buyer doesn't pay up, you'll have to foreclose on the property to get your cash out. While you should recover what you're owed (provided the buyer doesn't owe significantly more on the mortgage than the house is worth), the expense and hassle of the foreclosure process can be a lot to take on.

And obviously, not having all the proceeds of your sale at your fingertips can be a disadvantage too. If you need the cash for something else—like buying another house—seller financing won't be for you.

Evaluating a Buyer's Finances

If you do offer seller financing, pay particular attention to the buyer's financial picture. After all, if the buyer can't get a loan from a more traditional source, why should you be the one to extend tens of thousands of dollars in credit?

But don't jump to conclusions. Traditional mortgage financing has become harder to get than in any time in recent memory—it's not only the extremely financially strapped who are denied loans. Some people may have just had a bad financial patch, for example after an illness or divorce. And as adviser Mark Nash notes, "In today's market, even buyers with high down payments are getting turned down if they have 'marginal' credit—credit that would have qualified as 'good' just a few years ago."

But you'll need to evaluate for yourself. This means the buyer will need to provide you with information normally given to a lender. Ask for a summary of the buyer's total gross annual income from all sources, all debts, credit history, and cash reserves—plus back-up documentation like pay stubs, bank statements, and a credit report.

The first thing you'll want to figure out is the buyer's debt-to-income ratio. That's the proportion of the buyer's gross monthly income that is spent paying debts, including the upcoming mortgage payment. Traditional lenders don't usually want to see a buyer spend more than 28% of gross income on mortgage debt, with a maximum of 36% on all debts. This is a pretty reasonable requirement, considering that gross income is so often much higher than what most people actually bring home. You may allow a buyer with no debts other than the mortgage to spend more on the mortgage payment, but you'll probably still want to stay within the 36% upper limit.

Of course, this calculation is a little more difficult if the buyer is self-employed or doesn't have a regular salary—for example, is a commissioned salesperson. In either case, you'll want at least a couple years' worth of income history, so you can average out about what you should expect the buyer to earn going forward. (You'll want to pay special attention to the most recent months, to make sure the buyer's business seems stable.)

Also look at the buyer's credit score and report to find out what regular payments the buyer is already obligated to make and how good the buyer has been about paying money back in the past. The score you're looking for is the "FICO" score—so called because it's compiled according to a formula created by the Fair Isaac Corporation. That formula takes into account the buyer's history of paying debts, the amount the buyer currently owes, how long the buyer has been borrowing, how long the buyer has had any accounts, and the types of credit the buyer is currently using. The score will be a number somewhere between 300 and 850; the higher the better. Anything in the 700s is considered fairly strong.

The average consumer has 13 credit obligations on record at a credit bureau, including credit cards (such as department store charge cards, gas cards, or bank cards) and installment loans (auto loans, mortgage loans, student loans, and so on).

Source: myfico.com

Two of the three major credit reporting agencies (CRAs)—Transunion and Equifax —compile the information that creates a FICO score and allow consumers to access the score. (Experian will provide FICO scores only to lenders as of 2009.) They don't always have the same information on each consumer, however. To be extra safe, you may want to get reports from both. The easiest way is to ask the buyer to get copies and then review them. (The unscrupulous buyer could obviously alter them, so you'll have to decide whether to take that risk.)

You'll also want to think about how much money the buyer is bringing to the table. The larger the buyer's down payment, the more likely the buyer is to stick it out in tough times. At the same time, think about the value of the home—if you expect it to drop, you may worry that if the buyer doesn't pay up, you'll lose significantly should a foreclosure be necessary. But if you see an increase or stabilization soon, you can feel more confident even if the buyer's down payment is relatively modest.

You'll have to synthesize all this information and decide whether the buyer is an acceptable risk. Perhaps the buyer has a good reason for any negative information in the credit report—for example, a payment was late because it got lost in the mail—and is putting down enough cash that you're pretty certain a default is unlikely. In any case, big red flags—numerous late payments, defaulted loans, and the like—tell you that the buyer is a high risk to avoid, no matter how tempting it is to accept an offer, any offer. A solid deal that takes a little longer is still preferable to one that falls apart or worse, leaves you short.

Setting the Terms of the Mortgage

In a seller-financed deal, you must decide the terms on which you'll lend money to the buyer. You'll address these and other issues in two documents, including a promissory note—the buyer's written promise to pay you what's owed—and a mortgage or deed of trust, which provides security to back up that note. You'll want the documents to cover important factors such as:

- **Interest rate.** The interest rate should be comparable to what's currently available in the mortgage market (a mortgage broker should be able to tell you this). Keep in mind that if you're providing a second mortgage, the rate should be higher than it would be on a first mortgage, because in case of foreclosure, you'll get paid only after the first lender does. The higher rate compensates you for the additional risk; conventional loans also work this way.

- **Length.** Decide how long you'd like the loan agreement to last. As mentioned, it's common for sellers to finance the buyer's purchase for just a few years, at which point the buyer may refinance with a traditional lender.

- **Prepayment penalties.** Although often limited by state law, if you do decide to set penalties for the buyer paying the loan off early, you'll have to make sure they're clearly stated in your contract. You certainly don't need a prepayment penalty, especially if you'd be happy to receive the full payment at any time. But such a penalty makes sense if, for example, prepayment will negatively affect your tax liability.

- **When payments are due.** Spell out the date each month when the buyer's payments are due, and how the buyer should make them. A bank should be able to collect them for you in a "payment account," in which case you'll be notified if the buyer misses a payment. Also specify how much the buyer will pay each month, how the loan is amortized (a calculation that determines what portion of each month's payment is principal and what portion is interest), as well as how much the buyer will owe in a balloon payment if the loan is structured that way. Online calculators can help you create a payment schedule, such as those found at www.nolo. com/calculator.cfm (look for "How much will my fixed-rate mortgage payment be?").

- **The penalty for late payments.** You'll be leaving a huge loophole in your contract if it doesn't mention how the buyer will be penalized for late payments. Usually, this will be a reasonable late fee (again, state law may set a limit) due only after the payment is a certain number of days late, such as ten. You also need to spell out what your rights are if the buyer doesn't make the payment at all—for example, you might state that after 30 days, you can demand repayment of the loan in full.

- **The collateral.** Make sure the promissory note spells out that the mortgage or deed of trust serves as collateral for the loan. That way, if the buyer doesn't pay, you have the right to foreclose.

- **Whether the loan is assumable.** If the buyer decides to sell the house, can a subsequent buyer assume the same loan? At the very least, you want to reserve the right to evaluate the new buyer's finances and decide whether to allow the assignment. To best protect you, include a "due on sale" clause, meaning the buyer must pay the mortgage off if the property is sold.

These are just a few of the terms to make sure are covered. As you can see, these documents can be quite detailed and complex. You'll want an attorney's help to prepare them, or at least to review them if you create the first draft yourself.

Once the documents are complete, keep the promissory note (and give a copy to the buyer) and file the mortgage or deed of trust in the county recorder's office to put the world on notice that you have a financial stake in the property. This will prevent the buyer from selling the property without paying you off, for example.

Other Ways You Can Help With Financing

Seller financing isn't the only way to reel in a buyer who might have trouble borrowing enough to buy your house. Other options include letting the buyer assume your current mortgage and buying down the interest rate on the buyer's mortgage.

Arranging for the Buyer to Assume Your Mortgage

If your lender allows it, you can allow the buyer to assume your current mortgage—in other words, to step into your shoes and continue making payments on your behalf, on the same schedule. This may be an enticing deal for the buyer if your interest rate is significantly lower than what's available in the current mortgage market. When this book went to press, interest rates were at an all-time low. Should they stay that way, a buyer is more likely to get a mortgage from a traditional lender than to assume yours, which will probably be at a higher rate.

However, if a buyer is interested in assuming your mortgage, you'll have to make sure the lender allows it. Lenders usually permit assumptions only on adjustable-rate mortgages. You should be able to find the relevant information in your original loan paperwork.

And even if your loan is assumable, there's a major disadvantage to this strategy: You're still named on the mortgage. That means that if the buyer doesn't pay, you're ultimately responsible for making the payment. For this reason, loan assumption is best avoided.

Buying Down the Interest Rate

Another tempting incentive is for you to contribute cash with which the buyer can "buy down" the interest rate. There two ways to do this: a temporary buy down, in which you pay part of the buyer's interest obligation in the short term (say, three years), or a more permanent buy down. With the more permanent buydown, you essentially pay "points" on the buyer's mortgage. Points are an up-front cash payment, expressed as a percentage of the loan balance—for example, one point on a $200,000 loan is $2,000. The more points the buyer pays, the lower the interest rate, resulting in long-term

120 | SELLING YOUR HOUSE IN A TOUGH MARKET

savings over the life of the loan and smaller monthly payments. Another benefit of paying points when buying a home is that they're tax deductible for the buyer in the year paid.

EXAMPLE: Kelly and Brit need a $450,000 mortgage. They have two options, both 30-year fixed rates: one at 7.5% interest with no points and one at 7% interest with two points.

If they take the first loan, their monthly principal and interest payments will be approximately $3,146. If they keep this house and loan for 30 years, they'll pay about $682,722 in interest, plus the $450,000 principal, for a total of about $1.13 million.

With the second loan, Kelly and Brit are going to have to cough up $9,000 right away, to pay the points. Their monthly payments will be $2,994, around $150 less per month. Over the life of the 30-year loan, they'll pay around $636,791 in interest and points, which, plus the $450,000 principal, comes to about $1.09 million. The second loan offers them a long-term savings of almost $46,000.

If you help pay the points, it might even help the buyer get a loan he or she otherwise wouldn't have qualified for. And you'll certainly be helping the buyer save over the long term, plus reducing the buyer's tax liability in the year of the sale, when the buyer's cash reserves are probably already depleted.

Keeping Cash in the Buyer's Pocket: Cost Incentives

As you probably recall, buying a home is an expensive proposition. Just as the buyer is scrounging up every last dollar to make a down payment, a host of other new costs and expenses are popping up, such as inspection fees and moving costs. You can help defray some of the buyer's anxiety by offering to pay some of these costs yourself. There are many opportunities here, so think creatively.

Nonrecurring Closing Costs

Every sale involves closing costs that you or the buyer will pay just one time, such as fees for the mortgage broker, the title insurance premium, and real estate commissions. Exactly who pays such fees is often a matter of custom in the state or region where you live. Speak with a local real estate agent to figure out what's already expected of you.

But we're talking about traditions, not laws. So another incentive you can offer is to pay some of the closing expenses that would have normally fallen to the buyer. These may include:

- **Broker fees.** Mortgage brokers normally receive payments of at least several hundred dollars, in the form of various fees. You can offer to pay these fees so the buyer doesn't have to.

> **CAUTION**
>
> **Some fees are "junk."** Some mortgage brokers disguise bogus fees with names like "administrative fee" or "courier fee." Buyers can try to negotiate these fees away. But when you're paying these fees on the buyer's behalf, you won't be part of the buyer's loan negotiations, and so you'll probably get stuck paying them.

- **Title insurance and title search fees.** Whether the buyer or seller pays these fees (including the basic premium as well as the underwriting fees, namely for the title search) is typically a matter of local custom. If the buyer is normally held responsible where you live, you can usually cover these costs for around 0.5% to 1% of your house's purchase price. If it's been only a few years since you bought, ask whether this fee can be reduced by updating your original search.

- **Escrow fees.** These are fees paid to the escrow agent—the neutral third party (in some cases, an attorney) who will hold any payments until all conditions in the contract are met, then exchange the property title for cash. The agent's services usually cost several hundred dollars, though escrow companies will charge more for additional services like preparing the title report (which they are responsible for in some states).

> **What's all this adding up to?**
>
> According to a 2005 survey by bankrate.com, closing costs (not counting taxes, other governmental fees, or escrow fees) average $2,748 nationwide, with the highest fees in New York and the lowest in Wyoming.

- **Inspection fees.** Don't expect to choose the inspector just because you pay for one; the buyer should feel free to choose someone who's working totally on his or her side, to ferret out any problems with the house. But you can help by paying the inspection fees (or giving the buyer a credit for them—the buyer may want to write the check, to emphasize who the inspector is working for). Inspection fees usually run around $300 to $400, providing nothing unusual is needed.

- **Homeowners' insurance.** At closing, the buyer will be expected to prepay the homeowners' insurance premium, usually a full year's worth. If you offer to pitch in, expect this to cost somewhere from $500 to $1,300.

- **Home warranty.** Often confused with homeowners' insurance, a home warranty is actually a service contract, providing for repair and replacement of mechanical systems and attached appliances such as the furnace, plumbing, electricity, and more. If one of these breaks due to normal wear, the buyer calls the warranty company, which sends a repairperson. Instead of paying for the entire repair, the buyer pays a small fee, such as $50 or $100. Home warranties are entirely optional and cost around $300 to $900 per year, depending on the house. It's traditional in many states for the seller to foot this bill anyway, but if that's not the case where you live, you can offer to throw this in as an added bonus.

- **Property taxes.** Like homeowners' insurance, several months' worth of property taxes must usually be prepaid at closing. Taxes tend to make people grumpy, so the buyer would no doubt be delighted to unload this charge onto you. It will probably be at least several hundred dollars—the amount is based on the assessed value of the property and varies by location.

- **PMI.** If the buyer is putting down less than 20% of the purchase price, the lender is likely going to require private mortgage insurance, or PMI. The cost of PMI is tied to the amount of the loan and the down payment—a 15% down payment will require less for PMI than a mere 5% down payment, for example. The buyer will usually have to prepay up to one year's worth of PMI in an impound account, usually at a cost of several hundred dollars—so if you can come up with that amount, you'll make the buyer happy.

- **Mortgage payments.** You may offer to make the buyer's first mortgage payment, to ease the cost of transitioning into the new home.

- **Moving expenses.** While not part of traditional closing costs, all buyers have some costs associated with moving. You can help defray expenses and stress by offering to hire a moving company.

The buyer's lender may put a maximum on the amount of seller-financed concessions it will allow. For example, if the down payment amount is 10%, the lender may specify that the seller can pay no more than 6% of the sales price to the buyer through these types of incentives. (The lender just wants to be sure that the buyer has an actual investment in the home—that you're not just covering the buyer's down payment.) If you're willing to offer significant financial incentives, you may need to talk to a mortgage broker about what will fly with the lender.

TIP
No need to hand the buyer blank checks. If you decide to prepay any of these costs for the buyer, make sure you spell out a maximum amount. Rather than itemizing, you could also just agree to credit the buyer a specific amount for closing costs—say, $2,000.

Regular Monthly Expenses

Your home's next owner is going to have all the regular expenses you currently do. A buyer who is moving from a smaller home or rental may be unprepared for some of those costs. You may offer to pay a year or six months' worth of things like:

- **Utilities.** Paying for gas, electricity, water, DSL, the alarm system, or even cable in the first few months may help the buyer settle in and slowly replenish the bank account.

- **Association fees.** If your property is in a common interest development (CID) governed by a homeowners' association, this may be an added burden for the new owner. Temporarily paying these fees provides some time to adjust.

- **Services.** If you have someone who regularly mows the grass or cleans the house, consider continuing to pay the person to do the job for a bit, even though you no longer live there.

Cash Back at Closing

Some buyers aren't swayed by incentives—but may ask for actual cash back at closing. For example, a buyer may be willing to pay $25,000 more than your house is worth, but then say, "At closing, you have to pay me $25,000." The buyer can then use that cash for any desired reason—to make improvements to the property, buy new furniture, or go on vacation.

There's just one problem: These arrangements are of questionable legality, unless you explicitly tell the lender what you're doing. Otherwise, you're really defrauding the lender—that is, getting the lender to unknowingly issue a much riskier loan than appears on paper. And of course, if everyone were to do this, property values might shoot up artificially, because part of the "value" of your home is the portion going back to the buyer in cash (essentially, the amount the buyer overpaid).

In any case, it's unlikely any lender these days will allow a cash-back deal. (As discussed in Chapter 10, lenders will allow the buyer to be credited for repairs, but usually require the repairs to be made before escrow closes or demand the money be kept in an escrow account and disbursed to the buyer as the repairs are made.) Because the value of homes has dropped so precipitously, appraisers have become much more strict in assessing home values. (In the past, they had gained a reputation for practically rubberstamping the list price.)

In fact, at the time this book went to print, appraisers were facing possible federal regulations attempting to ensure their responsible behavior. Now, however, a home that's priced to account for cash back is unlikely to appraise at its stated value. If you fully disclose the cash back on your HUD-1 settlement statement (the form lenders use to lay out all the costs of the transaction), a lender is likely to reject the arrangement, recognizing the added risk and refusing to take responsibility for it.

Down Payment Assistance Programs: A No-Go

Another variation of cash-back schemes has been under recent scrutiny by the federal government. These so-called "down payment assistance programs," offered by companies such as Nehemiah Corporation and AmeriDream, were intended to help buyers raise the minimum down payments they needed to qualify for FHA-insured loans. Essentially, the seller would give the buyer a "gift" of down payment money, legitimizing it by transferring it through a third party, which collected a small fee. Now, FHA-insured loans can no longer be obtained using these programs.

More for the Money: Home Value Incentives

No matter how we try to escape it, we're all psychologically affected by the lure of a bargain. If you offer something "extra," it will make the sale more appealing than a comparable sale without the incentive. Or, if it's intriguing enough, it might get buyers to stop by and take a look who otherwise wouldn't have.

Notice we said "comparable sale." Some sellers think they can use incentives to distract buyers from artificially high asking prices. They think, "I'll give the buyer a plasma-screen TV, and I'll just increase the list price to cover the cost." If this is your strategy, don't bother. The value of the incentive won't be worth near as much to the buyer as the value of a reduced list price. According to broker and adviser George Devine, "I always scratch my head when I hear about home sellers offering things that are superfluous to the transaction, like a car or a trip to Hawaii. If they're going to pay for those things, why don't they just lower the list price? Especially because a higher selling price results in a higher documentary transfer tax and real estate commission."

TIP

Come on in, spend the night? To prove to prospective buyers how much they'll love living in the house, some sellers let them move in for 24 hours. No need to cater breakfast—but check with your real estate agent or attorney first, to draw up a mini-agreement about the arrangement.

Your Personal Goods

Your house itself offers an opportunity for some real incentives. As you may know, fixtures—those parts of the property that are affixed to the property and can't be easily removed—must be included in the sale. Anything that isn't a fixture is yours, however. That means you can take it with you when you leave.

If you're like many people, however, you may have purchased furniture or other items that specially suit the house you're in. Perhaps you bought a smaller "apartment-sized" couch and love seat to fit in your cozy living room, or a Mission-style dining table that blends perfectly in your Craftsman-style bungalow. A prospective buyer who sees these items may be impressed, and offering them as part of the package could seal the deal.

Beyond furniture, reasonable incentives might include appliances like an energy-efficient stackable washer/dryer that fits perfectly in a designated spot, a patio set that blends with your landscaped yard, gardening equipment, or exercise machines that are already assembled and ready to use in the basement rec room. In fact, when it comes to material goods, there's very little that you should hold onto with fierce determination, unless it has real sentimental value. Instead, think creatively about what will attract a buyer. (Just don't try to use the "incentive" to unload old furniture or junk you don't want to bother moving.)

Even if you don't initially offer these incentives, keep in mind that some savvy buyers may ask for some items when you sell. When Josh and Gillian

Here's one not to try:

A home builder in Florida reportedly offered prepaid college tuition plans for home buyers' children and grandchildren—but no one was interested.

received an offer on their house outside of Sacramento, California, in the dismal market conditions of early 2008, the buyer wanted a bookshelf, table and chairs, and pictures they'd bought just to stage the place. "We weren't about to let the deal die over a few pieces of furniture," Josh says. "We got very near our asking price, and we let him have the things he wanted—we'd already moved out, and it was more important to sell the house than to get our stuff back."

Upgrades and Credits

You may have decided to leave your house is in less than perfect shape when you put it up for sale. Maybe the carpet's worn, or the roof is getting old and will need to be replaced in a couple years. Instead of making these changes—particularly changes that aren't immediately necessary—you can credit the buyer with cash to do it, for example: "I'll give you $2,000 back at closing, for the carpet, and then you can choose your own carpet color" or "The roof's probably going to only last another year or two, so I'll credit $10,000 for that."

Arguably, you should just replace the carpet or roof yourself or discount the value of the property to account for these problems. But, particularly if these changes don't improve the physical appearance of your home (if the roof still looks okay, for example), a credit might be the better way to go. A change that's not physically obvious likely won't affect the buyer's interest in the property anyway. Offering a credit also saves you the hassle of getting the work done yourself, allows the buyer to make choices about how the change is made (perhaps choosing a metal roof rather than composite shingles), and gives the appearance that you're offering an "extra."

You can take this principle even further and offer upgrades to the home for non-necessary changes, too. Look at what the developers and builders of new homes do: When they want to attract buyers, one of the biggest incentives they use is upgrades. In fact, they'll try everything to avoid actually reducing the price: for example, replacing their standard kitchen (which might have white tile, oak cabinets, and vinyl flooring) with an upgraded version, with granite countertops, cherry cabinets, and tile flooring. For builders, such incentives make particular sense—they bring in buyers, keep prices stable across an entire development, and don't significantly increase labor costs (the builder has to install a kitchen anyway).

Still, if you offer extra cash with which to put in a granite countertop, replace a dated bathroom vanity, or upgrade existing closet doors, for example, you may get an undecided buyer off the fence. Just keep in mind that it's not as cost-efficient for you as it is for a builder—you probably didn't need to replace your countertop, in which case offering a credit to do so just adds on a new cost.

> **CAUTION**
>
> **Buyers aren't fooled by superficial "upgrades."** When Larry and Brooke bought their 1950s bungalow in an established neighborhood, it had been lived in by the same owner for many years, without alteration. The owner's children, who inherited the property, made some changes to get the place sold. One of the changes included installing brand new granite countertops on 1950s cabinetry, then adding new drawer hardware. "The look updates the kitchen somewhat," Brooke conceded. "But it's no disguise for an actual remodel, which we plan to do someday. We loved the house but we definitely weren't willing to pay extra for the countertop." Larry and Brooke estimated the value of the countertop and hardware at $5,000 and dropped their offer price by that amount.

A Deal for Later: Lease Options

Even in a cold market, where buyers have lots of good deals to pick from, there will be some would-be buyers who just aren't sure they're ready yet. Maybe a prospective buyer is finishing school and would love to settle down in the area, but figures it will take a few years to build up a down payment. Or perhaps the buyer is new to the area and is thinking about buying, but is still not quite sure.

To reel in such buyers, you may want to offer a lease option. Here's how it works. For starters, the interested party would lease your home from you, much like an ordinary rental. However, the lease would include the opportunity to buy the place at or by some set date in the future. As part of the deal, the prospective buyer would pay you something—either an up-front fee, or more likely a monthly amount, in addition to the rent—for the right to the option.

Lease options are particularly appealing to buyers who think the market is going to heat up soon but can't yet make a purchase. The buyer can lock in a low price, then decide a couple years later (by which time, according to the buyer's hopes, your house's value will have exceeded the preset price) whether to exercise the option and buy your home. Of course, as the seller, you'll get less on the deal than you would have by waiting and offering the property for sale at the higher value, years down the line. But it may ultimately get your house sold, and in the meantime, you get the regular monthly rent, plus whatever extra you and the buyer agree to for the value of the lease option. Or who knows, maybe the buyer will decide not to buy the place, and you can sell it at a higher price, plus pocket the money you were paid for the option.

Lease options do, however, have the potential to create a few headaches. For example:

- **You become a landlord.** Until the tenant exercises the right to buy, you're taking on a new, sometimes demanding role in life. You'll have to collect rent, maintain the property, buy necessary insurance, and more. And the tenant may not care for your house as lovingly as you did. In that case, if the tenant doesn't exercise the option, you'll get the property back in worse condition than before.

RESOURCE

Interested in more information about your duties as a landlord? You'll find it, as well as help writing a legally compliant lease, in *Every Landlord's Legal Guide*, by Janet Portman and Marcia Stewart (Nolo).

CAUTION

There are tax implications to a lease option agreement. One is that if you wait too long to sell, you may end up owing capital gains tax. Federal tax laws allow sellers who have lived in their homes for two of the last five years to exclude up to $250,000 gain or $500,000 if married filing jointly. But if you wait longer than three years to make the sale happen, you'll lose the benefit of this exclusion. If you're planning on doing a lease option agreement, discuss these and other tax implications with your tax adviser.

- **You can lose any appreciation in value.** If your house appreciates over the years it's occupied as a rental, but you've already set an option price, you won't get the benefit of the gain when the buyer decides to exercise the option.

- **You won't get much immediate cash.** While you'll get something for the value of the option, plus rental income, you won't immediately get the proceeds of your sale. If you need the money for other things right now—for example, to buy a new house—a lease option isn't going to work for you.

If you're planning to do a lease option, you'll need to draw up an agreement that reflects it. Get the help of a real estate professional or attorney. This agreement will probably include many of the typical terms of a standard lease, as well as language that specifically covers the option. Make sure it discusses:

- **Occupancy and related limits.** Spell out who will live on the property and include any limits (for example, that guests are allowed to stay for only a certain length of time, or that only a certain number of adults are permitted to live on the premises). Make sure the tenant can't sublet without your permission or assign any rights under the agreement (for example, bring in a substitute tenant or transfer the option to someone else).

- **Rental terms.** Spell out how much the rent will be, how long the lease lasts, how much the tenant will pay in rent, when the rent is due, and how you'll handle late payments and bounced checks.

- **Security deposit.** Most landlords require a security deposit upon signing the lease, from which the landlord can deduct for damage or nonpayment, particularly at the end of the tenancy. Make sure that you meet security deposit requirements in your state: For example, you may have to stay below a certain a maximum amount or keep the cash in a separate account.

- **Tenant's duties.** The agreement should specify what the tenant is responsible for, including any utility charges, maintaining the premises or notifying you of problems, paying for any damages he or she causes, and not violating any laws or causing any disturbances. Also make it clear whether the tenant can have pets and that the tenant's obligations to pay the rent exist whether or not the tenant lives on the property.

- **Your duties.** As the landlord, you have the responsibility of maintaining the property, and it will help avoid misunderstandings if your agreement mentions the scope of these duties (for example, by specifying that you have the right to enter the property in case of an emergency).

- **Option terms.** Specify how much the tenant will have the option to purchase the property for and when. Some options allow the buyer to purchase only on a given date; some on any date up to the given date. If the tenant can purchase any time, specify how much advance notice you'll be entitled to.

- **Option payments.** Make sure you spell out how much you'll receive for the option, and when.

The buyer may want to record the option—that is, file it in the county recorder's office. This is a fair request. Recording puts the world on notice of the agreement and prevents you from selling the property behind the tenant's back.

TIP
You may need to make legally required disclosures. If your state requires sellers or transferors of real estate to make disclosures about the property's physical condition, environmental hazards, and more, find out whether entering into a lease option triggers this obligation. In many states it does, meaning you'll have to provide these disclosures when you sign the agreement.

Get the Agents on Board: Agent Incentives

Your home's eventual buyer isn't the only person you can incentivize to get your home sold: You can also create incentives for your agent or the agents representing the buyers to make the transaction happen. For example, some sellers choose to give a cash bonus to a listing agent who sells a home quickly or to offer a higher-than-standard commission to an agent who brings in a buyer. Even vacations, cars, and other material goods aren't unheard of.

There's just one problem when creating agent incentives, however—agents (in most states, and if they're Realtors®) have a legal or ethical duty to provide the best professional representation to their clients, no matter what. That means they shouldn't be influenced by the extras you're offering. For this reason, we caution against these incentives. "An ethical agent isn't going to be influenced one way or the other," says adviser Mark Nash. "They're going to take the client to any house that could be the right one. And my experience is that clients are going to choose based on what's best for them, not how much their agent is being paid."

Still, there's nothing to legally prevent you from offering a higher commission or an added bonus to an agent. The reality is that this may increase the amount of interest in your property, which can help you sell more quickly. Just don't expect reputable agents to be so drawn by your added incentives that they'll push a buyer into making the purchase if it simply isn't the right home. A professional agent will be more focused on making a client happy than getting a little bit extra, knowing a good recommendation is more valuable.

TIP

At least make sure the buyer's agent is compensated fairly. Absent an unusual circumstance, that means the agent should get at least half the commission you pay to your own agent. As we explained in Chapter 4, make sure you know how much the agent is getting when you sign your listing agreement.

Market Like a Madman

Meet Your Adviser

Jaan Henry, broker/owner of Jaan Henry & Co., Realtors® in Montclair, New Jersey, and the owner of a relocation network of real estate agents across the United States

What she does: Works with buyers and sellers in residential and commercial real estate transactions in New Jersey's Essex, Morris, Union, Passaic, and Bergen Counties. She's been doing so for nearly 25 years, through every conceivable market, from wildly out-of-control seller's markets to slumps, slowdowns, and the recent catastrophe. With her relocation network, she places out-of-area referrals with other professionals whom she's known and worked with for many years.

• •

Favorite money-saving strategy in tough times: "Turn the heat down in your home! Also, for people planning to move into a rental, my advice—though it sounds counterintuitive—is to buy something instead, such as a condo. House prices will eventually go up."

• •

Likes best about her work: "It's a new experience every day; there's always something to learn. And I feel like I'm reinventing how to listen to each person, because everyone brings their own expectations to the table. I have a degree in social work and was a nurse before that, so this is very comfortable for me."

• •

Strangest thing she's seen homesellers do: "One flooded a basement just before the home inspection, because they got a better offer. They just turned a hose on. It didn't work—the inspector figured out what had happened. I was representing the buyer, who decided to go through with the sale anyway."

• •

Top tip for homesellers: "If you're selling because of a divorce, move out before people come to see the house, if you can possibly afford it. Visitors can feel the acrimony in the air."

A s we've hit upon again and again throughout this book, when selling in a tough market, creativity is key. In a sea of available homes, you want your house to stand out so that a buyer says, "That's the one!" Your own creative thinking can help make that happen. But the first step is to get the buyer to simply take a look at the property, and that requires extra creativity as you develop marketing materials and think of ways to grab buyers' interest.

Of course, your real estate agent, if you're working with one, will be the person primarily in charge of your marketing plan. (For purposes of this chapter, we're assuming you're working with an agent. If you aren't, also review the marketing strategies discussed in Chapter 5.) And agents come up with lots of creative ideas of their own, like the one who pitched a tent in the seller's front yard and kept his cell phone on so that he could show the place to buyers any time, 24/7.

But there's no rule that says you can't do some marketing of your own or check out what your agent is doing to make sure it's up to snuff. In this chapter, we'll give you some ideas for how to apply your creative skills toward doing some great marketing, hopefully getting your property in front of as many prospective buyers as possible.

> **CAUTION**
>
> **Typos happen.** Whether you or your agent prepares written marketing materials, it's best to run everything past a second—or even third—pair of eyes. We know of a case where the agent posted an open-house ad with the wrong address! Ask to see the major marketing material in advance.

Get Online

The vast majority of buyers look for homes online. It makes particular sense in a crowded market; if there are 100 homes for sale in a buyer's price range, the buyer probably doesn't want to go traipsing through every single one. Many homebuyers go to Internet sites that compile information about homes for sale, then tell their agents, "I already saw that one online—I couldn't stand the kitchen, so let's skip it" or "This one has real potential; let's check it out first."

Obviously, you want your house to be the latter—the kind that makes a buyer anxious for a personal visit. Here's how to best position your home online.

Get Your House on the Right Websites

One of the most important parts of making sure your house reaches potential buyers is ensuring it's on websites that buyers actually visit (not buried somewhere that no one ever looks). Here's where to start:

- **The local MLS.** The Multiple Listing Service (MLS) is a local or regional database of available homes for sale. Real estate agents nearly always post their clients' homes on the MLS, where other agents can access important details. The information from MLS systems is also often accessible, in limited form, to the public.

- **Realtor.com.** The data in the MLS may drive data to many other Web sources, too. The most prominent of these is Realtor.com, the website for the National Association of Realtors®, which aggregates listings from around the country and is a popular search tool for many potential homebuyers. The website includes only the basics of your listing and one photo, but your agent can pay extra to have multiple photos listed.

- **Other real estate websites.** It may be worth posting your property on other websites, such as those listed in "Most Popular Real Estate Websites," below. Many websites are aggregators that draw information from MLS systems automatically, which means you won't have to do anything extra as long as your house is in the MLS. Check with your real estate agent to be certain.

How about texting?

It seems to be the most popular form of communication for anyone under 30, and you can use it to get the word out. To utilize text messaging, you put a phone number on your yard sign or marketing materials. The buyer calls the number from a cell phone and gets an automatic text with a property description. It may not be the most popular tool just yet, but it could be the wave of the future!

Most Popular Real Estate Websites

According to *Business Week* magazine, these are among the most popular real estate websites:

realtor.com	homegain.com	remax.com
realestate.yahoo.com	zillow.com	ziprealty.com
move.com	century21.com	homes.com
hud.gov	realestate.msn.com	coldwellbanker.com

- **Your real estate agent's website.** Your real estate agent will probably have a personal website, which should include your listing. And if your agent is affiliated with a brokerage, your home should also appear on the brokerage's website. If either the agent or the brokerage highlight specific properties—for example, by listing them as "featured," find out what it takes to get the special designation.

TIP

Make sure your agent shares listings. If your agent is using an Internet Data Exchange (IDX) system, the listings should appear on the websites of agents who are also using the IDX. That increases your home's exposure. Ask the agent to confirm.

- **A website created specially for your home.** As explained in Chapter 5, some agents will create a website just for your home, such as www.123MainStreet. com. (Alternatively, the agent may just purchase the domain name and steer the site to the listing on his or her website.) This is a great opportunity to market your property without space limitations—that is, to post as many pictures as you want (MLS systems and other websites may limit this), or with as much detailed description as you'd like. If you're interested, find out whether your agent offers this service, or be prepared to do it yourself.

- **Your home stager's website, if you hire one.** Your home stager will have good reason to post pictures of your home; it's a great example of the work the stager can do and likely to appeal to prospective clients. But the increased Web exposure is good for you too. Maybe you'll nab a local buyer who's also selling and looking to hire a stager!

- **Craigslist.org.** This free service is popular for everything from selling cars to furniture to, that's right, houses. Your agent should be able to create the posting for you and may even be able to link in a series of photos or a virtual tour.

- **Local newspaper.** Your local newspaper may list homes for sale online, either through the local MLS or because you already bought a print classified ad.

- **Blog.** As explained in Chapter 5, it's easy and inexpensive to set up a blog where you can include pictures and a description of your home.

Make Sure Your House Looks Good On-Screen

The major advantage of viewing houses on the Web, from a buyer's perspective, is to see what the house looks like. And this works to your advantage too, because you can post pictures of your home's best features without having to include the parts you'd rather not highlight.

Your agent (if you work with one), will likely take the marketing pictures or hire a professional to do so. Either of these options is probably better than taking the pictures yourself, because people who do it frequently will know what works best. The major downside is that if it rains or is overcast on the scheduled day for photographing, you probably won't get the best possible shots. Try to build in some flexibility for rescheduling. Also make sure you'll get enough notice of the photo shoot to clean and prepare your house without having to fly into a panic.

Whether you take pictures yourself or hire someone to do it, make sure:

- **You've cleaned and decluttered.** Don't take pictures until you've taken the steps recommended in Chapter 3 to make your house buyer ready. If you've hired a stager, you obviously want pictures taken of the staged version, not the prestaged version.

Trade ya?

A few years ago, Kyle McDonald gained notoriety for trading his way from a red paperclip to a house in Kipling, Saskatchewan (Canada). As of the writing of this book, Kyle was ready to trade his way out of the home. To make an offer or see the story, visit http://oneredpaperclip.blogspot.com/.

- **It's light and bright.** Start by taking indoor pictures in the middle of the day, preferably on a very sunny day. Open all window coverings and make sure windows are clean, to let maximum natural light in. Outdoor shots usually work best when the sun is at your back, but still nice and bright.

- **You use a decent camera.** We recommend a digital camera for several reasons: First, it's easy to upload your photos; second, you can use the picture window to immediately see how your shots have turned out and discard those that don't work well; and third, you can get a fairly high-quality picture for a low price.

- **You choose the right angle.** A professional will have experience identifying the best vantage points; if you're doing the shooting yourself, you'll probably have to move around the room and try different angles.

- **You choose the right rooms and features.** Outside, you'll want a picture of the front of your home (without one, buyers will be suspicious your home is ugly, and may dismiss it quickly) and then a backyard shot or two if you have a nice patio or grass area or attractive landscaping. Inside, start with the room most important to buyers—your kitchen. If yours is modern and upgraded, you'll definitely want a shot or two of it. Then move to common areas buyers will want to see, plus at least a bedroom or two. And if your bathroom is particularly attractive, for example because it's larger than average or recently remodeled, you'll want a shot of that too.

One step up from pictures is a "virtual tour." Many real estate agents have the programs and know-how needed to create these "tours," which are really short, panoramic videos that allow buyers to get a moving picture of your home. For example, if you have a great room with kitchen, dining, and family room combined, a virtual tour allows the buyer a traveling view of the whole thing at once. (To see a sample, visit a virtual tour website such as www.justsnooping. com or www.visualtour.com.) Adviser Mark Nash highly recommends posting a virtual tour, which he says functions like "a 24/7 open house."

Make sure your agent plans to post multiple pictures of your home on the local MLS. (Many agents do this as a standard part of their marketing plan, but if your agent doesn't mention it, ask.) A good array of shots is more likely to hold buyers' interest than just one or two photos, which can be quickly rejected. And find out if your agent has multiple shots posted on realtor.com. As mentioned, this costs a little extra, but because so many people visit the website, it can really help drive traffic to your home.

Create an Enticing Online Description

In addition to the pictures, your Web posting should include a description of your property. In all likelihood, your real estate agent will write this, but ask to see it before it goes up. You're looking for:

- **Accuracy.** Obviously, if your house has three bedrooms and two bathrooms, that's how you'll want it advertised. Also check the lot size, square footage, address, directions, school district, and other factual details. (If your agent presents wrong information now, it could work its way into more official documents later—and buyers have sued sellers for things like overstating the house's square footage.)

- **Complimentary focus on your home's best features.** Your agent should hone in on what's best about your home, whether it's the open floorplan, remodeled kitchen, or picturesque back yard. If you think particular features bear special mention, discuss this with your agent. Maybe the agent has a good reason for putting the focus elsewhere. For example, an agent might suggest talking up the fireplace and hardwood floors in the living room, rather than the built-in bookshelves you adore, because those are features buyers are looking for.

- **Code words.** Real estate professionals use "code words" that carry specific meaning—for example, "motivated seller" or "bring all offers" tell other agents and buyers that the seller is anxious to sell and willing to consider offers below asking price. If that's true and you don't mind sharing the information with the buyer, no problem. But if you're more focused on getting top dollar than selling quickly, nix this language and ask your agent to decipher any other words that look coded.

- **The commission split.** As we discussed in Chapter 4, selling agents usually split the commission 50/50 with the buyer's agent. If you have anything different planned, it should be reflected in the listing.

How to Get the Word Out

Your real estate agent (if you have one) will take the lead in creating and implementing a marketing plan for your house. But don't just sit back passively—you can play an important role in this process, too. You might want to not only confer closely with your agent about strategy, but harness your own resources. For example, you could work on getting the word out to your own friends, who have perhaps appreciated the convenience of your outdoor kitchen at barbeques, or your neighbors, who know how wonderful it is to be located just a few blocks from a park or a school.

Here are some ways, both traditional and nontraditional. to tell the world that your house is for sale.

Create a Listing Sheet

In Chapter 5, we described what you need in a listing sheet—that is, a flyer you'll distribute to interested buyers, make available at any open houses, and perhaps put in a flyer box on your yard sign (discussed below). Your agent, if you're represented, should create the listing sheet for you. (To get an idea of what's usually on the agent's listing sheets, ask for a sample first.) Ask that the agent confirm the sheet with you before making hundreds of copies.

The basic principle to remember is that the listing sheet isn't just a recitation of your house and its features. It's an advertisement, designed to draw in buyers. It should highlight your home's best features, but leave enough mystery to draw buyers in. And it should be descriptive, not just factual. For example, instead of stating "backyard garden and spa," you might say, "outdoor retreat with Zen garden and luxury spa" (unless it's just an ancient hot tub with algae growing in it). The sheet should include pictures—in color, to maximize contrast and appearance—and enough text to provide the basics, but not so much that it looks like a book no one has time to read.

For more information on creating a listing sheet, see Chapter 5.

Get Other Agents Excited About Your House

Your agent isn't the only one trying to sell your house—in all likelihood, local buyers' agents are just as eager to find the perfect match between your property and their clients. But a lot of properties are on the market these days, so you still want to make sure your house gets their full attention and stays on their minds.

Start by making sure your agent does a special open house for other agents (sometimes called a "broker's tour"). This is an opportunity for the real estate community to come look at your property (usually on a weekday) and for each agent to decide whether it could meet any of his or her clients' criteria. If it does, the agent will come back for repeat visits and bring clients along.

These open houses can create a buzz about your house. A number of agents will be in there all at once, and many of them already know each other. They'll be sharing opinions with the raucousness of movie reviewers, from "This kitchen will sell the place," to "Oh no, what were they thinking with the fuchsia bathroom tile?" If your house is well priced and looks great, they may be vying to bring purchasing clients in quickly.

Speaking of repeat visits, make sure it's easy for agents to make them. The most practical thing is for your agent to leave a lockbox on the front door—a small box that can be opened with a special key or a code, which professional agents will have. With very little notice, this allows prospective buyers to come over and have a look around. This works well any time of day, so if you're at work, a buyer's agent can just call and ask you for permission to take a client on a tour. Of course, it also requires you to keep your house in good shape at virtually all times—something we recommend anyway, when you're trying to sell.

Adviser Jaan Henry says a lockbox is far preferable to the alternative—that you're home and open the door for sellers. "Without the convenience of a lockbox, it's not super easy to show your house, and it's going to get passed by," she says. "If you're doing the showing, you'll inhibit the buyer, who's not going to go poking around in the closets and really getting a good feel for the house."

CAUTION
Make sure your agent promptly returns calls and other inquiries.
Even with a foolproof system for allowing potential purchasers to look at your home, you also need an agent committed to getting them in the door. Before hiring, discuss with your agent how long it will take to respond to buyer inquiries. Also make sure your agent solicits feedback from other agents after visits and shares that feedback with you.

Hold a Public Open House

Open houses are a standard in most real estate agents' marketing portfolios, but beware: They rarely lead to sales, especially in cold markets, where there aren't as many buyers even looking. As adviser Jaan Henry points out, "They are very, very expensive to advertise in the paper, and most of the folks coming through are just lookers not ready to make a decision or other homeowners checking out the competition."

Nevertheless, in a tough market, keeping maximum traffic going through your house can increase the odds of a sale—and there's still the possibility that someone who visits an open house will come back to buy or make a recommendation to someone they know is looking. Unless your agent points to specific reasons that an open house makes no sense in your local market, it's worth the limited amount of time it takes. Just recognize that if you get few visitors, it's probably not worth doing another one; that's an indicator that in your market, you're probably better off having your agent allocate marketing time and money elsewhere.

TIP
Make sure your agent advertises your open house in your MLS listing. That way, other agents and prospective buyers know they can come visit.

Your agent should plan to hold at least one open house of your home, and possibly more. (You can always cancel a scheduled open house if you find an acceptable offer beforehand.) Your main responsibilities before the open house are all the last-minute cleaning and decorative tasks described in Chapter 3. On the actual day of the open house, you'll just need to get yourself, your family, and your pets out for the day. Your agent is the best one to interact with visitors.

Hold a Specially Themed Open House

The standard open house isn't your only possibility. Creative home sellers have come up with variations on the theme—sometimes called "extreme open houses"—based on their house's particular features. For example, we've heard of sellers of a home with obvious remodeling needs or potential holding an open house at which they arranged for architects, contractors, and other experts to talk with guests about what's possible and feasible. Other sellers with large backyards good for entertaining have held barbecues, or arranged for musicians to entertain visitors. Creative sellers have hired professional chefs to create (and serve) gourmet dishes to show off a remodeled kitchen, or have put up an art or antiques show in coordination with a local gallery or shop.

Events like these can admittedly cross the line into being gimmicky and definitely aren't something to spend a lot of money on. Nevertheless, it's worth giving some thought to how you might make your open house stand out, either at the public open house or the broker's tour. And if there's already an architect, chef, musician, or other relevant professional in your circle of friends and family, why not create an event that people will make a special effort to attend?

Get Into Print Advertising

Whether its worth your agent's limited advertising budget to get your property into physical print is questionable and depends on where you live. In most places, users will go to the Web first. Even if they later pick up a description of your house in a classified ad, it's not going to have the same impact that multiple images would.

However, some newspapers still have robust real estate sections, often with a special pull-out on weekends. If your house can be featured in one of these, it might be worth paying for. But if all you're getting is a three-line classified ad, you'll find it tough to draw much attention, especially if the ad is full of cryptic abbreviations. If you're going to do such an ad, focus especially on appealing adjectives that will help buyers picture what they can't see.

Like newspapers, other print media—magazines, local circulars, and the like—rarely sell homes. Your agent may still use these forms of advertising, but don't expect print media to sell your house. Serious buyers rarely rely on them. And why should they, when the Internet allows them to get a lot more information from the comfort of their own homes, even if they live hundreds of miles away? Also, their agent will most likely be doing some searching for them, using the MLS. Given that, you're better off working with an agent who will focus primarily on promoting your house online.

Put Up a Yard Sign

A yard sign is a simple yet effective tool for letting others know your property is for sale. As adviser Jaan Henry points out, "People who are happy in a neighborhood always have friends and colleagues and relatives they'd like to have closer to them. So having a sign is a strong, low-cost marketing tool." Your agent should provide the sign (if you don't have an agent, see Chapter 5 for more tips on putting up signs).

If your agent has created a custom website for your house, you can give the URL on a "rider"—the small plaque that hangs off the bottom of the sign. Riders can also be used for information like open-house hours. Also make sure the relevant phone number is visible; if it's a custom extension number (with a prerecorded message, for example), be sure the extension is also on the sign.

TIP

Have a designated phone line. Some agents have a phone line or extension devoted to a specific property for sale. This allows interested buyers to call and usually to hear a prerecorded description of the property and, perhaps, to leave a message to get more information.

The sign should be visible from the street (that is, perpendicular to it) so anyone driving by can read the details—most importantly, the contact information. (While you'll get some people walking by, most local foot traffic isn't house hunting.) Also consider having a flyer box to hold your listing sheet (discussed above). Just recognize that you'll need to keep it regularly stocked. Ask your agent to leave extra copies at your house, so you can refill it as needed.

Offer Incentives to People You Know

It isn't unheard of to meet the person who buys your house through a common acquaintance. In fact, using your current personal contacts can be a good way to augment your agent's marketing efforts.

Start by letting your immediate circle know you're putting the place up for sale. Pass around your listing sheet, website address, or other property description. Then send an email or letter to everyone you know who may be of use—most likely, family and friends located close by. Explain that you're selling and are interested in finding someone through your current contacts. Ask them to forward the listing sheet or other information to anyone they know looking for a home in the area.

There are a couple ways to really broaden this search. The first is to offer a financial incentive, for example, "We'll give $500 to the person who introduces us to our buyer." Just make it clear that the $500 must be split down the line—if your brother sends it to a friend who sends it to a cousin who forwards it to the buyer, you'll split $500 between the three of them, not pay them $500 each. This financial incentive should be large enough to entice your friends and acquaintances to cast a wide net.

Another strategy is to open the search up to anyone and everyone you can think of, from your dentist to the gardener to the neighbor you've never met. Encourage others to pass the information along, and make sure it's easy for any interested party to reach your real estate agent or you (if you're unrepresented).

Send Postcards to Your Neighbors

If you have a flyer box in front of your house, you may find it's quickly depleted—not only by house hunters, but by curious neighbors. Don't feel annoyed; instead, see it as an opportunity for more guerilla marketing.

To save your flyer box and get a little more strategic, try sending out a postcard to neighbors in the blocks right around you. If your agent has an open house planned, mention that on your postcard. Otherwise, the postcard is simply a way to give your neighbors a heads up and a reference to your website, if you have one. Some real estate agents may do this as part of their marketing plan.

Hold a Neighbors' Open House

Your agent will probably plan on doing an open house for local agents and another for the public. You might also talk to your agent about holding an open house just for the neighbors (with or without your agent's presence). This lets people nearby know that they're free to come poking around your place. And you may get some good feedback.

Consider serving light snacks or drinks or offering up a prize to the person who gives you the most useful sales preparation advice. Put balloons outside the front door to attract attention and make the place feel festive and welcoming. Just know that you can keep the mood light, since you're not actively trying to sell to someone who lives in the neighborhood. (Of course, if a neighbor shows interest, be sure they know how to contact your agent.)

Hit Your Target

As you take the steps recommended above, we suggest you keep someone specific in mind: your buyer. While you obviously don't know who that is yet, you can probably make some educated guesses. In a small condominium in the middle of a busy city and close to public transportation, your buyer is most likely to be a working professional, possibly single. On the other hand, a rambler in a suburb with excellent schools and a park nearby is likely to draw a family with school-aged children.

Why bother thinking about this? Because you may be able to tailor some of your marketing material to your audience. While you can't expect to cover every prospect, it's worth spending a little time thinking about who will be coming through most frequently and making the marketing material—not to mention the house itself—as attractive to those buyers as possible.

> **CAUTION**
>
> **Don't discriminate.** Federal (and often state or local) fair housing laws prohibit you from discriminating against potential buyers based on factors like race, color, national origin, religion, sex, familial status, or disability. While you may market your house with the general idea that it will probably appeal to a certain type of buyer, your marketing materials shouldn't say that's who you're seeking.

How Would You Describe Your House's Most Likely Buyer?

Start by thinking about your home's attractive features, then who will be drawn to them. Here are some objective factors; no doubt, your home itself will reveal similar clues:

- **Size.** A house with many bedrooms will probably draw families with children; a smaller house may draw empty-nesters or young singles.

- **Schools.** A good school district is most important to families with children (though it holds general appeal because it affects resale value).

- **Location.** In a suburb or small town, expect buyers looking for a quiet place to live. In the city, you may get more people seeking cultural activity and nightlife. Proximity to recreational facilities, public transport, and places to work will also influence your pool of likely buyers.

- **Layout.** A house with stairs, for example, will have less appeal for a retiring couple or for families with small children, who may prefer the convenience and safety of one level.

- **Condition.** If your house is completely remodeled and needs no fixups, it's just right for someone looking to spend time doing other things— perhaps a driven, working professional looking for something low maintenance. On the other hand, if your house needs some sprucing up and the price reflects it, it will probably find appeal more to people on a budget (such as first-time buyers).

- **Price range.** If your house sells for less than the median where you live, you're more likely going to be dealing with first-time buyers breaking into the market. This is especially true if you're also in an area with lots of other first-time buyers—for example, a subdivision of small, "starter" homes.

By using this list and thinking of other special features about your home, as well as the demographics of where you live, you should be able to narrow in on a few groups likely to buy your house. It may be that your house appeals to multiple groups: For example, its location in a good school district might make it ideal for families with children, while the condominium ownership might make it ideal for single professionals who travel a lot.

Match Your Marketing to Your Buyer

What's the secret to making your marketing material attract the folks you identified as likely buyers? Consider customizing your:

- **Written descriptions of the property.** Although your marketing material must accurately reflect your home, you also want it to highlight the features of greatest interest to your prospective purchasers. If, for instance, you're selling a small, two-bedroom house in a vibrant, diverse neighborhood, you may want to mention the flexibility of the second bedroom, which could be used for an office, guest room, or nursery.

- **Ad placements.** For example, in an area likely to draw families looking for good schools, placing an ad in a neighborhood paper or even at the school might be appropriate.

- **Online presentation of the property.** For a family, you may want to show pictures of the "quiet, tree-lined street." For buyers looking for a bustling community, don't forget to include a shot of the busy weekend farmer's market in a nearby park. Or, if your home may appeal to unrelated folks living together—perhaps because it's a townhouse with two master suites, or in a college town—be sure to include pictures of both bedrooms and bathrooms.

- **Property staging.** Talk to your stager about who you think will be visiting the house, and how the staging can boost the house's appeal to those people. For example, if you live in a thriving artist's community, you might stage a semifinished garage to look like an artist's studio.

- **Buyer incentives.** As we discussed in Chapter 6, you may want to consider offering incentives to your prospective buyer. If you're in a starter home, seller financing may look particularly attractive to first-time buyers who have a hard time qualifying for a loan. If you're in a more upscale neighborhood, prospective buyers may already own their own homes and be more appreciative if you're willing to accept a home-sale contingency.

- **Time of sale.** Obviously, if you need to sell, you need to sell. But if you have some control over when it happens, targeting certain times of year may be effective. For example, in a college town, turnover may be highest at the end of summer or beginning of fall, when students are just returning or arriving. (Along with students come professors, support staff, and perhaps graduate or mature students who may already be thinking about buying.) And families will want to move before the school year starts, to help kids adjust to new schools. ●

Adjust Your Strategy If You Need To

Meet Your Adviser

Stephen Fishman, a Bay Area attorney, tax expert, and author

What he does: Stephen has been writing about the law for over 25 years. Among his many books are *Every Landlord's Tax Deduction Guide; Easy Ways to Lower Your Taxes: Simple Strategies Every Taxpayer Should Know* (co-authored with *USA TODAY* personal finance columnist Sandra Block); *Home Business Tax Deductions*; and *Working for Yourself: Law & Taxes for Independent Contractors, Freelancers & Consultants* (all from Nolo).

Favorite money-saving strategy in tough times: "Somebody gave me this suggestion and I think it works: Watch less television. I'm not just talking about the hundreds of dollars you can save by getting rid of cable TV, but there's also less exposure to consumption and advertising. Less television also encourages you to fill the time with something more active (not passive) and more interesting … perhaps starting a new business or hobby that may provide satisfaction and even have some value."

Likes best about his work: "I like the intellectual challenge and I like being able to work at home any time of the day or night. But what I like best is that I get to work on projects from start to finish instead of working by the hour for someone else!"

Top tip for homesellers: "I think the best advice I would give to a seller is to know your home's value. Many sellers have unrealistic ideas of home value. Websites like Zillow.com can give you an idea of what local homes are selling for and then you need to compare and revise that number based on any pluses (the value of your renovations) or minuses (unrepaired damage, and so forth) associated with your home."

I n a down market, selling your home can sometimes take a long time—
anywhere from a month to a year or more. But what if you're watching
other houses in your area sell faster than yours, or you urgently need to
get yours sold soon? This chapter will guide you through the most likely next
steps, including:

- dropping your price

- reevaluating other parts of your strategy, and

- taking your house off the market for a while and relisting later.

Of course, the longer you wait, the more difficult your economic situation
may get—especially if part of your original reason for selling was that you
needed the cash from the house or were having trouble paying the mortgage.
So we'll also take a quick look in this chapter at two ways to make staying in
your home affordable, including:

- renting out a room, and

- taking out a reverse mortgage (if you're age 62 or older).

Dropping Your Price

If your house hasn't sold within a reasonable time—particularly if not many
people are even showing up to take a look—the first thing to consider is
reducing your price. It can be hard to accept that your home may not be
worth what you'd hoped. So, start by accepting that you probably can't
evaluate it objectively on your own. You'll instead need to listen to what
would-be buyers are quietly telling you by turning away, get some more data
on the latest market conditions, and adjust your price accordingly.

How long is reasonable to wait before considering a price reduction?
Your first clue is the number of days the house has been for sale. Ask your
real estate agent to check the MLS and tell you the average number of days
properties are on the market in your area. If you've already passed that time
without any offers or real interest, you should probably begin to wonder
whether the price is the culprit.

Finding Out Whether Your House Is Overpriced

No matter how great your house is, or how fair you thought you were being in setting the price, the market may be telling you that buyers simply aren't willing to pay that price. Adviser George Devine notes, "Historical pricing data is good, but not perfect." In the end, it's buyer demand that determines your house's "true" value.

What Were They Thinking?

In 2006, when the local real estate market was hot, Alayna's neighbors put their house on the market for $415,000. It was an unbelievably high price, as comparable properties were going for around $375,000.

A few months later, the property still hadn't sold. They dropped the price to $385,000—a huge adjustment, but still over market value. And the market was beginning to show signs of weakening. They left the sign in the front yard for nine months, then finally took it off the market.

By the time they relisted it the next summer, values had plummeted. The new asking price was $349,000, but by then the market was very competitive, and it still didn't sell. As of the writing of this book, the list price had dropped to $269,000. They're still living in the house now. If they'd been more realistic from the beginning, they probably could have gotten their final asking price and then some.

Even if your price was appropriate at the time you listed, market values may have gone down since. Perhaps you've already noticed the trend yourself, as nearby "For Sale" signs have started sporting "Price Reduced" riders, or as you browse MLS listings and find better and better bargains.

To figure out what's really happening, ask your real estate agent to run another comparable market analysis (CMA), or if you're selling FSBO, do one yourself. Also visit local open houses yourself (or with your agent), to get a sense of how actual houses on the market compare to yours in price and other features. Finally, ask for your agent's honest opinion. He or she has been in the field for awhile and is working with others, too. If you're open to a truly objective analysis, your agent should be ready to give it. As adviser Nancy Atwood says, "Prepare yourself for a reality check!" (In fact, studies show that most homeowners have trouble accepting how much their house's value has dropped.)

> **TIP**
>
> **Change happens fast.** Adviser George Devine warns, "It's easy to get hung up on thoughts like, 'But my neighbor sold a similar house just recently for lots more!' In a fluctuating market, even six months ago isn't so recent. In fact, even if your neighbors were to agree to sell their house today, by the time the deed is recorded and the price becomes public information, that information is already a month old."

Setting a New Price

If you discover that your price is now too high for the market, you'll definitely need to reduce it and consider lower offers than you were perhaps willing to before.

> **How about $50 for a raffle ticket, instead?**
>
> Yes, some creative sellers have tried raffling off their houses. Unfortunately, raffles are illegal in many states and tough to organize. Auctions are a more realistic possibility, either live (see www.auctioneers.org) or at online sites like eBay.

Your price adjustment needs to be big enough to get buyers' attention—at least raise their eyebrows, if not drop their jaws. That's especially true if your house has sat on the market long enough to be stigmatized. Real estate professionals and potential buyers may be dismissing it as unworthy of any buyer's attention. They'll imagine, for example, that it has hidden problems that turned off other buyers or that you've stubbornly refused to accept lower, more reasonable offers.

The upshot is that you'll probably have to go lower than the price you would set if you were just now putting the house on the market for the first time. Use all the information you've gathered to make your adjustment: the CMA, information garnered by looking at your competition, and your agent's opinion as to how big a reduction will grab people's attention.

Of course, that may mean slashing your price many thousands of dollars, which can be emotionally difficult. But keep your eyes on this basic truth: The lower you go, the faster your house will sell.

> **TIP**
>
> **Are you close to the edge of a lower price point?** If your adjusted price can drop you into the lower price point—for example, by going from $389,000 to $374,000, which will move you from the $400,000 to the $375,000 price point—you'll generate even more interest.

How to Excite Buyers With Your New Price

Once your house has been listed for awhile and buyers have passed it by (perhaps without even looking at it), they may not give your new price the attention it deserves. Here are some ideas for regenerating interest:

- **Update your MLS listing.** Have your agent change the MLS listing not only to reflect the new price, but to highlight it. For example, you might include phrases like "Just reduced!" or "Motivated seller!" Just be aware this may make some buyers think that you're getting desperate, which could end in lowball offers.

- **Do new open houses.** If you've also spruced the place up a bit (more on that below), talk to your agent about scheduling another broker's open house. That lets the brokers see for themselves that your changes, combined with a price reduction, make the place more saleable. Then consider doing another open house for the public, to see if you can't bring in some folks who weren't interested before. Be sure your open house ads draw attention to the reduced price.

- **Update your listing sheet.** Instead of just deleting the old price and putting in the new, consider crossing out the old one so it's still visible, showing the new bargain.

- **Get a new sign rider.** Your agent should have no trouble getting a small sign to hang off the primary sign (a rider) that says "Price reduced" or something similar.

Don't expect immediate results—only the best deals get snatched up quickly in a cold market, even after a significant reduction. Just keep the average days on market in the back of your mind. If your house still doesn't sell or even generate much interest after hitting that number, that's a good time to consider another reduction. Eventually, some buyer is likely to sit up and notice what a great deal you're offering.

RESOURCE

Having trouble paying your mortgage while you wait? Get in touch—quickly—with a housing counselor approved by the Department of Housing and Urban Development (HUD). Such counselors usually charge little or nothing and can help you review your financial situation and contact your lender. Visit the HUD website at www.hud.gov or call them at 800-569-4287. Also check out *The Foreclosure Survival Guide,* by Stephen Elias (Nolo).

Short Sales:
When You Can't Sell for Enough to Pay Back the Mortgage

As we discuss price reductions, one obvious lower limit is the amount that you still owe your lender on the mortgage. But if the house isn't worth what you owe and you really have no choice but to sell, there's another possibility, called a "short sale." It allows you sell the house for a lower price, so long as your lender agrees to accept that amount and cancel the loan even if the proceeds don't cover what you owe. (In some cases, the lender may make you assume part of the loss as well.)

You'll have to approach the lender with an actual offer in hand. The lender won't be happy about this, but might agree if it's clear that even after the hassle of a foreclosure (which can take months), it's not going to recover the full amount you owe. (If you have more than one lender, however, getting them all to agree may take a minor miracle.)

> ### What's the name of that saint again?
>
> You've probably seen the regular newspaper stories on this one: Many people believe that if you bury a statue of St. Joseph the Worker in your yard, he'll help sell your house faster. (In fact, the companies that sell these say that real estate agents are among their best customers!)

> **CAUTION**
>
> **Don't try to hide the short sale from potential buyers.** Adviser Jaan Henry says, "I've encountered situations where the seller didn't mention the short sale until well into the transaction, which is completely unfair. If the buyer assumes it's going to be a straightforward sale, they won't know to plan their time around bank delays and may spend money on inspections and other fees for nothing. I've started asking listing agents of homes I'm going to show whether it's a short sale, so the buyer can be prepared before walking in the door."

At first glance, a short sale sounds like a great way to say goodbye to a house that's become a burden, with potentially less of an impact on your credit rating than foreclosure (or bankruptcy) would have. But there are disadvantages. For one, you'll have to work hard to convince the lender that you don't have any other alternative nor access to any other sources of cash and that you're not just going to sell the house cheap to a friend or relative. Adviser Joel G. Kinney urges, "Start the process as early as possible by getting in touch with your bank, which will want a lot of financial information from you."

And then you'll have to cope with the lender's playing a role in your negotiations with the prospective buyer. The lender may, for example, insist on lower real estate agent commissions (such as 4% rather than 5%), and refuse to allow any of the sale proceeds to be used for inspections, paying off liens, or certain other closing costs.

And finally, you'll need to get the lender's approval in time to avoid the buyer losing interest, which can be a challenge in some parts of the United States. You may be in line behind many other homeowners requesting the same thing. Expect a wait of at least two weeks, and more likely around two months. Mark Nash says, "Here in the Chicago area, it's been taking at least two months to get bank approval. I think the banks themselves are waiting to see whether a better offer will come in." Jaan Henry adds, "My experience is that it can take as long as six months to work anything out with a bank, and also that it may never get worked out, which can be devastating to a buyer who has been on hold all that time."

Your tax liability is also a concern. If any of the debt that your lender is writing off was not actually used to buy or improve your house—for example, you took out a home equity loan to pay college tuition—then whatever amount you don't pay back is considered taxable "forgiven debt." (The debt used to buy or improve your home is also forgiven debt, but a special law protects you from federal tax liability on that portion.) Your only way out is to either file for bankruptcy or to prove that you are legally insolvent at the time of the short sale; in other words, that your total debts are higher than your total equity in your home and personal property.

> **TIP**
>
> **Don't stop the short sale approval process if the buyer pulls out of the deal.** Joel G. Kinney advises, "Try to keep pushing the bank for approval based on the previous agreement. Then when you relist, you can speed the approval process, particularly if your new offer is at the same price and terms."

Figuring Out What Else Might Be Wrong

Sometimes, price isn't the main or only issue. According to adviser Nancy Atwood, "If there have been a lot of visitors to the home, then the property is probably priced correctly, but something else is wrong." Perhaps the remaining amount of repair work has put people off, your efforts at cleanup have fallen by the wayside lately, or there's something else you haven't thought of—like the fact that there's new construction across the street and buyers want to wait to see what will be built. Here are some ways to find and fix the problems.

Get Outside Input

You're probably stumped about why your house isn't selling. But you're not without help: Ask others for input, and you're sure to find some willing to give it. Do you have friends or family members who haven't seen your house yet? Invite them to a mock "open house," in which you fully stage and prepare your house as if for real buyers. Hand out a questionnaire asking each visitor to explain what they liked most and least about the house and to offer suggestions. Serve some food, and make it a proper party.

Of course, it's too bad you can't eavesdrop on what actual prospective buyers visiting your house have been saying—but wait, your agent can do the next best thing. Jaan Henry explains, "I get ongoing feedback by contacting real estate agents who've shown the house to prospective buyers. I thank them for showing the place and ask what the visitors thought and whether they have any further interest in the property. Then I pass the information along to my client, no matter how painful. Sometimes the visitor was put off by something as simple as the toilet seat having been left up after a child forgot to flush."

And here's one more possible source of outside feedback: If you've staged your house yourself or have doubts about the work your hired stager has done, you might also hire another stager on an hourly basis, to come in and suggest improvements.

The one outside source *not* to talk to is another real estate agent, if your listing agreement with your current agent is still in effect. That can seriously muddy the waters, especially if the new agent believes you're hiring him or her and perhaps takes steps to bring in buyers. (As explained above, it's fine for your agent to make that contact.) But if you're selling FSBO, you may be able to pick real estate agents' brains for free, by asking what they'd suggest if you were to turn over representation of your house to them.

Have a Talk With Your Agent

This being a tough market, there's no sense rushing to put the blame on your agent. Nevertheless, you may need to light a fire under an agent who is feeling the same fatigue that you probably are by now. Start with a sit-down meeting where you look over everything that's been done so far, evaluate what's worked and what hasn't, and develop a strategy for going forward.

Realtor® George Devine advises, "Put your agent to work—say, 'Speaking honestly, why hasn't this place sold? Show me recent sales data, and explain to me what's happening in the neighborhood.' It's not enough for the agent to hold another Sunday open house and stand in the kitchen smiling." And if you haven't already, consider offering your agent the incentives described in Chapter 6.

TIP

Was the agent overly enthusiastic in writing your house's marketing copy? Adviser Nancy Atwood explains, "If the marketing materials have been over-embellished—you know, the classic thing of describing a matchbox-sized house as 'cozy,' or saying the house is 'close to shopping' when there's a strip mall across the street—it can create disappointment or annoyance when people actually visit. They may lose interest based on that emotion alone. On the other hand, the description could be so unappealing that nobody is interested; but that rarely happens."

If you've followed the advice in this book, you should be able to tell better than anyone whether your agent has done a good job. Is your agent marketing your house properly? Does he or she promptly respond to you and to buyers and make buyers feel comfortable during showings? Has the agent explained the process to you well enough that you've been able to make informed decisions about price and the rest? Be fair—if your original price wasn't realistic and against your agent's advice, and you've since lowered it, the fact that it didn't sell earlier isn't the agent's fault. But a good agent will be nimble enough to think up new ways to draw prospective buyers to your house after the reduction (though no one can make them buy).

However, if you really think your agent hasn't been aggressively working to get your house sold or hasn't been making the process easy for you or prospective buyers (for example, because the agent takes a long time to return phone calls or doesn't return them at all), you may need to reconsider your choice of agent. If you're coming to the end of your listing agreement anyway, the simplest step is to say no to signing up again.

Even if the agreement is still in force, however, it is possible to fire your agent. But because of the potential hassle, we suggest saving this for the absolutely worst circumstances, like an agent who does virtually nothing. A better alternative is to first talk to the office's "managing broker"—the agent's boss—who will be motivated to help you work things out.

If you're determined to end the relationship as quickly as possible, first check your agreement for the terms that allow you to do this. You may, for example, need to give the agent sufficient notice, usually about 48 hours. And you may have to pay the agent if you sell the house within a certain period of time after terminating the agreement. Of course, we're assuming that there's been no action on your house—firing an agent just to get out of paying a commission, when it's the agent's work that brought in the buyer, is completely unethical. (One way to deal with this issue is to get a list of all potential buyers who were shown the house during the period of the listing, and then name them as "exceptions" to any subsequent listing for a specific period of time, typically two to four weeks or more.)

Try Something You Haven't Before

We've given you lots of marketing ideas in this book, but you probably didn't implement every last suggestion. So maybe it would help to go back and add one or two more ideas to the mix. For example:

- **Can you advertise someplace new?** See Chapter 7 for advertising ideas.

- **How about holding an open house at an unusual time?** By opening your house on a weekday, or better yet, a weeknight, you may bring in some visitors who either happen to be busy on Sunday afternoons or find it convenient to swing by your house on their way home from work.

- **Does your house really look its best for showings?** If you've held off on something like painting or removing the toys from your child's room, taking the added step now might be worthwhile. Follow the advice in Chapter 3.

- **Consider offering some new incentives.** Hearing that you'll cover some closing costs, which many buyers pay out of pocket, can cause ears to perk up. For these and other financial incentives, check out Chapter 6.

Or you might come up with something even more unusual, based on your house's unique features. Mark Nash describes an event he helped another agent plan: "In the winter holiday season, the Chicago market tends to slow down quite a bit. And this particular house, despite being a large place in an upscale suburb (perfect for entertaining), wasn't getting much traffic at all, much less offers. So we came up with the idea of using the house as a venue for a charity fundraiser. The sellers chose a children's cancer charity, and about 150 people attended. The charity was delighted to save the cost of renting a venue, and last I talked to the selling agent, the amount of showing had picked up afterward."

TIP

How about swapping houses? Tired of trying to sell their houses, some homebuyers—usually living in different states—have turned to swapping. Of course, the two houses need to be in the same price range. Find out more on websites like GoSwap.org or OnlineHouseTrading.com.

Taking Your House Off the Market Temporarily

You may feel like you need a break from trying to sell your house, and the house might benefit from a break, as well. Adviser Jaan Henry says, "Some practitioners are now taking the house off the market after three to four months." Later, when you relist your house on the MLS, it will get a new number, making it appear fresh and new. (The old number incorporates the date and year you first listed, creating a dead giveaway that you're having trouble selling.) Of course, to really freshen up your new listing, you may need to lower the price, based on the criteria described earlier in this chapter, and perhaps make other changes.

In fact, taking your house off the market may not be the only way to have it relisted on the MLS. In some areas, a price change or listing with a new agent will also qualify you. (Your agent can tell you the local rules.) But don't rely too heavily on such methods, which are controversial and seen by some as manipulative. As adviser Mark Nash points out, "Buyers are pretty savvy, and they'll do a property history search and find out that the house has been on the market ever since the original list date. That can look like you're being deceitful, in which case the buyers will wonder what else has been undisclosed, and you'll damage their trust from the beginning."

So how long should you wait before putting your house back on the market? "I would suggest a minimum of 30 days," says Nash.

Also consider the season during which you'll be relisting. Starting out during winter isn't the best idea, because the market is at its coldest then—literally and in terms of buyer interest. Houses don't show well when the trees are bare and days are short. You'll risk your house going stale all over again. Springtime usually brings in the most buyers. If possible, wait until April (after tax day, so people aren't distracted) or later to relist.

Your other option is to take the house off the market for the long term and to consider the alternatives discussed in Chapter 9.

Keeping the Cash Flowing

Continuing to own your house wasn't what you'd planned, and you're no doubt going to feel the financial impact. If you've already moved out, see Chapter 9 for suggestions on renting the house out. If you're still living there, here are a couple of quick ideas for easing the financial burden: either renting out a room in your house or, if you're older than 62, applying for a reverse mortgage.

Renting a Room in Your House

Finding someone willing to rent space—even if it's a basement room or a small bedroom in your New York co-op apartment—can be more feasible than you'd think. This is particularly true if you live in a college town or an area where rents are high. It's a bit like the old-fashioned system of bringing in boarders, except that you don't have to cook for them (unless you want to). Of course, it's easiest all around if you can offer each renter a separate room, as well as a separate bathroom. And you'll need to check your state or local ordinances on what constitutes habitable space, as well as any rules set by your homeowners or co-op association limiting your ability to rent the place out.

True, you'll be losing some privacy and sharing some common space. Depending on your house's layout, you and your tenant(s) may be cooking dinner side by side, eating at the same table, and soaking up sun on the same back porch or fire escape. If you have children who are old enough to stay home alone, there may be times when your tenant is the only one in the house with them. And when no one else is in the house, your tenant has access to all of your worldly goods.

But there's good news: You can apply tighter screening criteria than other landlords would (for example, if you prefer to live with a person of the same gender, that's okay—although you can't ask advertisers to put this in print). And a good tenant comes with more advantages than just the monthly rent check. You might enjoy the company, the help entertaining the kids, and having someone to keep an eye on the house and pets when you're away. For more information, including important tips on tenant screening, see *Every Landlord's Legal Guide*, by Marcia Stewart, Ralph Warner, and Janet Portman (Nolo).

Any added expenses that you take on—such as advertising costs, repainting and repairing the rental room, and more—are likely to be tax deductible, just like in any other landlord/tenant situation. (See "Tax Benefits of Renting Your House," in Chapter 9.)

Not only that, but you'll be able to deduct a portion of your fixed or general expenses, such as your

> ***Flight crews and pilots often rent rooms within homes!***
> They may need an affordable "crashpad," or a bed to call their own when staying in another city. (The airlines don't always cover these costs.) For details, and places to advertise, go to www.airlinecommuter.com, www.crashpads.com, www.craigslist.org, and www.airlinecrew.net.

property taxes, mortgage interest, and utility and garbage bills. The easiest way to calculate what portion of these is deductible is, according to adviser Stephen Fishman, normally to figure out what portion of your house is dedicated to rental use and then apply that percentage to the total costs. Talk to a financial or tax pro for a personal analysis.

In figuring out how a renter could add to your budget, however, don't anticipate having the room occupied year-round. Expect a little higher than the average vacancy rate where you live (Chapter 9 explains how to find this out), because it's more likely that you'll end up with a tenant in transition (perhaps recently graduated, divorced, or new to the area and looking for more permanent housing).

To maximize flexibility—yours and the tenant's—using a month-to-month tenancy agreement rather than a lease makes the most sense. The month-to-month arrangement allows you to end the tenancy on short notice, typically 30 days, without having to prove that the tenant did something wrong—perhaps because you just didn't get along very well. With a lease, you can't terminate the tenancy until the lease runs out or the tenant has violated its terms or the law. Of course, the tenant, too, can terminate the relationship with short notice—what you gain in flexibility you lose in locking in a tenant for a set period of time for a set rent. But this makes your home more attractive to a wider pool of potential tenants, who may be looking for that flexibility.

> **CAUTION**
>
> **Don't go without a written agreement.** As adviser Janet Portman explains, "While this relationship may seem casual, the potential for misunderstanding is great—and you don't want to be having arguments over the breakfast table. Your written agreement should spell out more than an ordinary one would regarding certain rights and responsibilities—making clear, for example, that the tenant is responsible for buying bathroom supplies, must clean up the kitchen within a certain time after creating dirty dishes, cannot park in your garage, may use the laundry equipment but not after 11 p.m., and more."

One last financial issue to take care of will be to call your homeowners' insurance company to explain your intentions and make sure your policy will cover you if your tenant unintentionally damages your property, causes injury to others, or gets hurt at home. It's a good idea to require any roomer to buy renter's insurance, which will cover the tenant's belongings if they're damaged in a fire or other accident (your policy won't cover them) and will also step up if your tenant causes accidental damage to your property or to other people. Of course, your own policy will cover you if the tenant causes damage and might cover if his or her acts injure others, but you'll be better off if any settlements or judgments come from the tenant's insurance company, not your own. Not all states allow landlords to require renter's insurance, however; check with your insurance broker or representative.

Reverse Mortgages for Seniors

If you're approaching retirement or have already stopped working, you may have been hoping that the sale of your home would be a valuable source of financial support. And your retirement accounts may have dropped in value recently, leaving you wondering where to go for cash.

A reverse mortgage might help, if you're 62 years of age or older and the existing mortgage on your home is fully or nearly paid off. (You must pay off your current balance as part of the process.) Unlike a regular mortgage, a reverse mortgage means that the lender pays you (either as a one-time lump sum, in monthly payments, or a line of credit). You're basically taking out a loan against the equity in your home.

You don't have to pay the loan back until you sell the home, move out permanently, or die. Within a year of that time, the loan, plus accrued interest and possibly other fees, must be repaid from your house's sale proceeds (your equity). If there's any profit left over, you, or whoever will inherit from you, can keep it. If, after your death, the sale proceeds are not enough to cover the loan, the lender won't go after your heirs for the difference. What if the house doesn't sell at all during the one-year period after your death or departure? The interest owed will continue to build up, and technically, the lender could foreclose. But they're reportedly unlikely to do that, so long as a good-faith effort is being made to sell the place.

Unfortunately, the amount you can borrow using a reverse mortgage may be less than it would have been in real estate boom years, since it depends partly on the value of your home and the amount of equity you have in it. (It's also based partly on your age at the time you apply for the loan, but the older you are, the more you can borrow—they figure you have less time in which to use up your equity.) There's some good news even in the current market: The maximum amount that homeowners can borrow using a reverse mortgage has recently been raised, to $625,500 (2009 limit).

Another issue with reverse mortgages is that the closing costs can be high. Between $13,000 and $20,000 is typical. This includes a 2% maximum origination fee paid to the FHA, as well as a fee to the lender and the usual mortgage fees for a title report, appraisal, and so on. Because of this, experts advise not getting a reverse mortgage unless you plan to stay in the house for at least two more years.

Before the mortgage industry meltdown, reverse mortgages were widely available from both private lenders and Fannie Mae. However, the main source of reverse mortgages now is the FHA, with the Home Equity Conversion Mortgage, or HECM. For more information, go to www.hud.gov and click "Owning," then "Reverse Mortgages," then "All About Reverse Mortgages." ●

Don't Sell Yet; Rent It Out

Meet Your Adviser

Janet Portman, attorney, author, Nolo editor, and syndicated columnist

What she does:	Her "day job" is managing Nolo's editorial department, where she oversees work on all books and software and writes about legal issues related to landlords and tenants. Among the many books Portman has authored or co-authored for Nolo are *Every Landlord's Guide to Finding Great Tenants* and *Every Landlord's Legal Guide* (about which the late, esteemed real estate expert Robert Bruss said, "On my scale of one to 10, this outstanding book rates an off-the-chart 12").
Favorite money-saving strategy in tough times:	"Resist the temptation to rent quickly to the first plausible applicants. Although you may lose rent while you hold out for acceptable tenants, in the long run, you'll come out ahead by avoiding costly repairs occasioned by thoughtless tenants; turnover expenses that result from having to terminate flaky tenants; and worst of all, legal fees associated with evicting tenants who turn out to be nightmares."
Likes best about her work:	"I like best what landlords like least: Landlord-tenant law is incredibly complex, involving not just the basics (security deposit laws, privacy laws, repair requirements), but employment law (many landlords hire managers), discrimination law (which governs what you can and can't say, do, or write in many situations), and even biology (mold! bedbugs!). With so many issues to understand, it's no wonder that landlords often get into legal hot water."

Strangest thing she's seen sellers do:	"Treat tenants like their friends—in every respect. While it's great to be on friendly terms and to be kind and humane when your tenants come upon hard times, it's a mistake to lead them to believe that you will always deal with them as you would your best friend. When your tenants become your friends, be prepared to sacrifice either the friendship or the health of your business."

• •

Top tip for homesellers:	"If you're selling a home that's occupied by renters, go out of your way to secure their willing cooperation, by offering a reduction in rent, assuring tenants of reasonable "showing" days and times, and even supplying house cleaners or gardeners if you want the house to appear even a little bit staged. Consider waiting until the lease is over (or give month-to-month tenants proper notice terminating their tenancy) if you suspect they'll take this opportunity to sabotage your sales efforts."

Maybe, despite your best efforts, now just isn't the right time to sell your house. This can be hard to believe, when houses were flying off the shelves, figuratively speaking, just a few years ago. But if a willing buyer just doesn't seem to be in the cards, it may be time to take down the "For Sale" sign.

Of course, this can create a major problem: If you've got your heart set on moving or have moved out already, you've also got an empty house on your hands. A possible solution is to rent out your house until the market recovers and house prices rise again. In this chapter, we'll help you explore that option, starting with whether it's economically feasible.

> **CAUTION**
>
> **If you live in a condominium or other common interest development, check the rules first.** Some CIDs place numerical limits on how many units can be rented or ban renting altogether. And they're known for vigorously enforcing these rules—in at least one case, to the point of having a homeowner arrested for renting out his home.

If you're horrified by the thought of being a landlord, don't worry: You don't have to do it forever. In fact, for maximum flexibility, you could bring in tenants on a month-to-month basis, which you may end on short notice (usually 30 days). We'll give you some tips to explain what tasks the job entails, plus resources to learn more.

> **CAUTION**
>
> **Still planning to buy another house?** Expect lenders to approach your loan application with caution. They'll want to make sure that you can handle two mortgages at once, plus all the other expenses associated with owning two homes. (Of course, they'll give you credit for anticipated rental income.)

How Much Rent Your House Will Bring In

While your main goal may be to wait for house prices to rise enough to sell, you'd no doubt like to earn some rental income in the meantime—at least enough to cover your mortgage. Unfortunately, this isn't guaranteed. So don't just guesstimate your monthly income or hope for the best. Do the research and run through the analysis below to determine whether you'll make enough money each month.

Calculating Rental Income

Wouldn't it be nice if you could just add up your expenses for the property, tack on a little extra for profit, and call the result your monthly rental amount? Well, it doesn't work that way (except by coincidence). The local rental market largely sets the prices, based on how many properties are available and what amount tenants are willing and able to pay. That's why many landlords must settle for rental amounts that don't actually cover their costs, hoping long-term appreciation in property value will ultimately lead to profits.

To figure out how much you can charge, look at local ads for comparable properties of the same size and condition, in the same neighborhood and school district. When figuring out which properties are comparable, pay special attention to issues on the minds of renters. The following features have a big impact on how much the landlord can charge:

- **Size.** Compare your house to houses with the same number of bathrooms and bedrooms and roughly the same square footage.

- **Location.** Nearby public transport is a big plus, as is proximity to shopping and commercial areas.

- **Security.** The safer your street and neighborhood, the more people are likely to be willing to pay to live there.

- **In good repair.** Even if it's otherwise in good shape, a house with ongoing maintenance issues—perhaps a nearby creek that often floods or being so old that everything is falling apart—may put off tenants if they can find better-maintained properties for the same price.

- **Layout.** If the house is likely to be shared among roommates, you can charge more if the property provides more privacy—for example, two master suites with private bathrooms.

Also, when setting your rental rate, consider whether you might be willing to allow pets or charge a lower security deposit in trade for a higher rent. Conversely, if there are a lot of vacancies in your area, you might want to set your rent below market rates to draw a larger pool of prospective tenants.

> **CAUTION**
>
> **Got a luxury house?** Don't expect it to bring in correspondingly high rent. That's because your pool of prospective tenants will be unusually small. Those who can afford your monthly rent can probably also afford to buy a house.

Visit other rentals to see how yours stacks up. There's no need to be undercover about it: Identify yourself as a new landlord researching the market, and you may find a fellow landlord who's eager to share tips and stories.

After figuring out a likely market rent, your next task is to check out the local "vacancy rate"—the average amount of time rental properties sit vacant each year—usually expressed as a percentage. This is a step many new landlords skip, but it's important. Your home will not be rented 100% of the time, and you should account for that when deciding whether it's economically feasible to rent it out.

A real estate or property management company should be able to tell you what percentage of local rental houses like yours are sitting empty now or at any given time. You can also get a sense of the likelihood that the rate will change by considering factors like whether your area is growing or declining economically (so that employees will either need new housing or are moving out), and whether the falling real estate market is increasing the demand for rental units. It tends to have this effect, since many people are nervous about buying or have left a house due to foreclosure. Nationwide, a vacancy rate of up to 10% of the year is not uncommon, according to U.S. Census Bureau figures.

Putting it all together, you should be able to come up with an annual dollar figure that your house is likely to command—the monthly rent figure times 12, minus expected vacancies. (To be on the safe side, assume that your vacancy rate will be the same as the average where you live, even if you expect to have a long-term renter.) Divide that by 12 to get an average monthly figure.

When Can You Raise the Rent?

After you're in full swing as a landlord, you should keep an eye on changes in your local rental rates by watching the ads and talking to local real estate management experts. If rents go up, you may be able to renegotiate a raise at the next lease renewal or, if you have a month-to-month rental agreement, within the next month or two (depending on your state's requirements for giving the tenant advance notice). Local rent control laws, if any, will also affect when and by how much you can raise the rent.

But don't assume raising the rent means a little extra cash each month—it could mean an earlier than anticipated vacancy instead. Rent hikes can alienate good tenants, who may decide to move elsewhere. It does make sense to raise the rent to current market value when someone new comes in.

Subtracting Expenses

You know that keeping up your home isn't cheap, between annual expenses like the mortgage, homeowners' insurance, and property and other taxes. As a landlord, you may need to add some expenses, for property management services if you decide to use them, accountant fees if your finances get complicated, plus extra maintenance costs. (Tenants tend to be harder on houses than owners and blind to minor maintenance issues until they become major.)

TIP

You may need a business license. Some cities or localities require that all landlords—or those whose properties have a minimum number of units—register their properties, pay an annual license fee, and possibly undergo a property inspection. Check with your city for details.

Draw up a budget, estimating what it will cost to keep your property as a rental. The worksheet below will help with this task. We've broken it down so that you enter monthly figures—of course, you'll need to fiddle with some of the numbers, for example, dividing your annual property tax payment by 12.

Our expense worksheet also includes some categories that you may not be able to estimate yet, such as gifts (for example, flowers to your tax accountant for dealing with your shoebox of receipts). For now, leave these blank if you can't imagine paying them—just keep in mind you may be filling them in later, and use those amounts to calculate expenses in later years.

Monthly Property Expense Estimate	
EXPENSE DESCRIPTION	**AMOUNT**
Advertising and tenant screening	$
Local transportation	$
Out-of-city travel, meals, and lodging	$
Cleaning and maintenance	$
Homeowners' insurance (if not included in mortgage payment)	$
Legal and other professional fees (accountant, property manager, and others)	$
Mortgage payment (principal and interest, plus property taxes and insurance, if included)	$
Other loan payments	$
Repairs	$
Appliances and furnishings (irregular, but major, expenses such as a refrigerator)	$
Supplies (for your own office use and for the rental property)	$
Income tax	$
Property tax (if not included in mortgage payment)	$
Utilities and phone (if not covered by tenant)	$
Gifts and entertainment	$
Licenses	$
Homeowners' association dues (in condos and some developments)	$
Landlords' association dues, if you choose to join one	$
Educational publications, subscriptions, and memberships	$
Tools and equipment	$
Construction and improvements	$
Other miscellaneous expenses	$
Total estimated expenses	$

> ⓘ **CAUTION**
>
> **Costs can mount if you're unable to make regular visits to the property.** As Amy, who began renting out a house she owned in Texas before moving to California, explains, "My property tax bill recently went up significantly, and I decided it wasn't worth the time and expense to fly from California to Texas to appeal it. But if more surprise costs like this come along, I'll probably have to either raise the rent or sell."

Estimating Profits

Continuing with the simple calculations, let's estimate whether the rent will cover your costs. Do that by filling in the chart below:

Estimated Monthly Rental Profit or Loss	
Expected monthly rental income (based on "Calculating Rental Income," above)	$
Minus estimated monthly costs (based on "Monthly Property Expense Estimate" worksheet, above)	– $
Equals monthly profit or loss	= $

This chart will tell you whether you stand to bring in monthly income by renting out your house. If so, great. But even if you'll be renting the house out at a loss, keeping the house could be worthwhile if you ultimately earn more selling a few years down the line. You'll have to make an individual determination based on whether you can handle the loss in the short term and the prospects for a turnaround in real estate prices in your area. Keep your eyes on both the national and local news, stay in touch with your real estate agent about your house's comparable value, and regularly reevaluate whether continuing to rent makes sense.

Another thing worth considering is the value of your own time. We can't calculate that for you, but we will discuss some of the tasks that go into being a landlord in this chapter.

Tax Benefits of Renting Your House

The rent that you'll receive is considered income and subject to tax. However, you may be surprised at how much the various deductions associated with renting out a house can lower your taxable income. (Don't confuse tax deductions with tax credits, however, which lower your actual tax liability, dollar for dollar. For example, if you make $80,000, a tax deduction of $10,000 will lower your taxable income to $70,000, whereas a tax credit of $10,000 means you'll actually pay $10,000 less in taxes.)

Below, we'll set forth the basic formula used by landlords calculating taxable income, to give you a sense of how much you'll personally be able to deduct. Here's what you'll do:

- **Add up the property's gross income.** This is mostly rent received over the year.

- **Deduct (subtract) start-up expenses.** Start-up expenses are any expenses incurred before offering the property for rent, so long as they're related to getting the business up and running. Examples include costs of researching and investigating the rental market; how-to books; classes and seminars; attorney and accounting fees; licenses and repairs to get the property ready to rent; office supplies including telephone, paper, and notebooks (but not equipment and other long-term assets); and advertising. You can also include any other operating expenses paid before offering the property for rent, such as for landscaping and gardening services, property maintenance, and utilities (excluding utility connection fees). Startup expenses under $5,000 can be deducted in full—after that, it gets more complicated.

- **Deduct operating expenses.** Operating expenses include most of the day-to-day costs you'll face as a landlord, such as interest payments on mortgage loans, other loans, credit cards, property and other taxes, professional fees, license renewals, ongoing insurance premiums, homeowners' association dues, your local transportation expenses, out-of-town travel costs, property repairs, maintenance and cleaning, the costs of making your property accessible to the elderly or disabled, office supplies, education, advertising, and tenant screening.

- **Deduct depreciation.** Over time, certain types of property start to get worn out and lose value—or at least, that's how the IRS looks at it, resulting in a special "depreciation" deduction. Examples of common depreciable assets for landlords include the rental house and its structural components, personal property bought for the house (such as appliances, furniture, and carpets), and personal property bought for use on the rental property, such as tools and equipment. You can't deduct the cost of these items in the year you buy them, but must take depreciation deductions over the "useful life" of the property, called the "recovery period," using an IRS schedule. For example, your house will have a recovery period of 27.5 years. Calculate the dollar amount to depreciate by comparing the following two numbers. First, note the house's fair market value (determined by researching comparable house sale prices and not counting the land, which doesn't deteriorate and isn't depreciable) on the date of the change from personal use to a rental property. Then calculate your own adjusted cost basis in the property on that date (that's the cost to you to purchase the property, plus the cost of any improvements, reduced by certain allowed costs like closing costs). Your depreciation figure will be the lesser of the two amounts.

> **CAUTION**
>
> **Watch out for "depreciation recapture."** Your annual depreciation deductions will be subtracted from the house's tax basis. When you sell, the basis gets subtracted from the sales price to determine if there was a taxable gain or loss. Thus, the depreciation taken will reduce any loss and increase any gain. Any gain up to the amount of depreciation taken in prior years is taxed at a 25% rate, not the normal capital gains rate of 15%. Any gain left over is taxed at normal capital gains rates.

- **Deduct any Section 179 expenses.** Section 179 of the federal tax code lets business owners deduct the entire cost of certain long-term personal property (property that doesn't get used up within a short time, such as machinery or furniture) in one year, rather than having to depreciate it (take proportional tax deductions over the life of the property). Section 179 is subject to an annual maximum and limited to the total of your profit from all your businesses and your salary (if you have one). Unfortunately, because of its various rules and exceptions—including the fact that you can use it only for personal property not contained in your rental property—this section is nearly useless for landlords.

The result is your taxable income, or the amount the IRS will ask for a bite of.

Calculating Taxable Rental Income	
Annual gross income from property	$
Start-up expenses (education, office expenses, advertising costs, etc.)	– $
Annual depreciation	– $
Section 179 expenses (if any)	– $
Total taxable income	= $

TIP

We're assuming you'll really be acting like a business owner. If you're merely a property "investor"—essentially, a person in the business of buying and holding property to make money, without doing much else—you won't have access to as many tax deductions. For example, if you're lax about placing ads and the property sits vacant for months at a time, the IRS could classify you as an investor (and make you pay penalties and back taxes if you claimed business-owner deductions). The key is to earn a profit by actively running a business—that is, work at it regularly, systematically, and continuously. Hiring a property manager to take over much of the activity still counts, for IRS purposes.

It's entirely possible—especially if you recently bought your house—that you'll be able to wipe out all your taxable rental income with your expenses, and not have to pay any tax at all on the rental income. (Of course, you'll need to keep good records of every penny spent.) If you actually show a tax loss on the property, you may be able to deduct the loss from other income, but this gets more complicated. It's governed by what are called the passive-loss and at-risk rules, which we don't cover in this book.

RESOURCE
For in-depth information on the topics mentioned in this section, see *Every Landlord's Tax Deduction Guide,* **by Stephen Fishman (Nolo).** And for personalized advice and an estimate of your tax savings, consult an accounting or tax professional—you can deduct that expense, too.

Congratulations, You're a Landlord

Don't worry, you won't need to quit your job to start renting out your house. Many landlords deal with the issues of property ownership in their spare time. However, you will have to educate yourself about what's involved, and dedicate time—sometimes large blocks of time—to tasks like the ones described below:

- **Preparing the property for renting.** Every landlord needs to make sure that the house meets your state's requirements for fit rental housing and is attractive to renters, before putting it on the rental market. Fit rental housing has adequate weatherproofing, plumbing, safe electrical systems—the basic attributes that people expect to find in a home. Fortunately, you probably took care of most of the needed tasks already, when preparing your house for sale.

- **Deciding on your rental policies and drafting a lease.** A well-written lease is crucial for establishing rights and responsibilities between you and your tenant. A clear lease will help prevent misunderstandings and disputes or at least give you a structure for dealing with them. The lease should comply with federal, state, and local laws and specify your personal preferences regarding pets, subletting, how you want the rent delivered, and much more. Plan on spending an hour or two deciding on your rental policies and creating a lease with the help of resources like the ones mentioned below.

- **Advertising the property and holding open houses.** The period before you get your house rented is the most time demanding, with long stretches required for tasks like holding an open house or showing the place to individual visitors.

- **Screening tenants.** This includes meeting prospective renters in person and gathering and reviewing rental applications and credit reports, as described further below.

- **Coordinating tenants' move-in.** Plan on a meeting to sign the lease and a visit to the property to show the tenant things like how to use the dishwasher and which potential maintenance issues to keep an eye on.

- **Responding to any neighbors' complaints about the tenants.** Hopefully, you won't have many of these, but you should give your contact information to the neighbors and quickly respond to any complaints. Neighbors can be a great set of eyes and ears, especially if you don't live nearby.

- **Doing annual inspections of the property and taking care of regular maintenance and repairs.** How much time you spend on maintenance depends on the condition of your house and whether you hire a property manager (who can take maintenance calls and coordinate repair people). At the very least, however, you'll want to make an annual visit just to check out the property's condition—tenants don't always notice or inform you when something on the property is deteriorating.

- **Responding to emergency maintenance and repair calls.** Yes, you might get some midnight, "We've been hearing water running under the house and the crawl space has turned into an ocean," calls. You can minimize the chances of receiving such calls by keeping on top of maintenance.

- **Collecting rent and following up when rent is late.** With a good tenant, this will be easy—and vice versa.

- **Going through eviction proceedings when necessary.** If you end up with a tenant who doesn't pay the rent or violates the lease terms, you'll probably have to go to court to file an eviction lawsuit. This is a huge bother and time-consuming—just another reason to devote time and energy to your tenant-screening procedures.

- **After a tenant leaves, starting all over again.** You can minimize the number of turnovers by signing yearlong leases, but you must be prepared for more frequent turnover if tenants unexpectedly leave.

You can hire a property manager to handle many of the responsibilities above—in fact, it's probably your best choice if you're moving far away.

Of course, the fees will reduce your income from the property. Property managers normally charge about 10% of your monthly rental income for their services. And that doesn't count their handling any additional tasks, such as terminations or evictions, for which you'll pay extra. Plus, you'll still need to keep in touch with the property manager and occasionally visit the property yourself.

RESOURCE

How will you do it all? Details on handling landlord matters are available in:

- ***First-Time Landlord: Your Guide to Renting Out a Single-Family Home,*** by Janet Portman, Marcia Stewart, and Michael Molinski (Nolo), which introduces you to the whole panoply of start-up issues, including practical and legal matters
- ***Every Landlord's Legal Guide,*** by Marcia Stewart, Ralph Warner, and Janet Portman (Nolo), a comprehensive guide including handy form rental applications, leases, and rental agreements and other useful worksheets and documents, and
- ***Every Landlord's Guide to Finding Great Tenants,*** by Janet Portman (Nolo), an in-depth guide to advertising, screening, and notifying applicants, with over 40 forms.

How to Find Good Tenants

If you've never rented out property before, you may find it hard to imagine how you'll reel in good tenants; that is, ones who will not only pay the rent on time, but take good care of your home until you're ready to sell. Conversely, you want to know how to avoid tenants who will cause problems by not paying the rent, trashing the property, or bothering the neighbors. Fortunately, other landlords and the legal system have created standard procedures and processes for you to use in bringing in new tenants, which we'll preview here.

TIP

Don't take down the staging just yet. A nicely staged home can attract high-paying tenants in the same way that it attracts home buyers. Unless the rented furniture costs are killing you, leave it up.

Advertising Your House for Rent

A little word-of-mouth among your friends or colleagues may be all you need to find the perfect tenant, particularly if the rental market is tight and you have a competitively priced house. For wider choice, however, you can:

- Put a "House for Rent" sign in front of the house, on a nearby corner or sidewalk, or in one of the windows.
- Post flyers on neighborhood bulletin boards.
- List with a local home-finders' service that provides a centralized listing of rental units for a particular geographic area.
- Advertise in a local newspaper.
- Work with a local real estate broker who handles rentals.
- If you live in one of the many areas served by Craigslist (www.craigslist.org), use that free online service (or other local online services you may find).

The method of advertising that will work best depends on your house (its rent, size, amenities, and location), your budget, how much competition you're facing, and the type of people who will likely be your tenants (such as students versus families).

TIP

A picture really is worth a thousand words. One of the great advantages of online advertising services is that you can post digital photos of your rental, inside and out.

Showing your house to prospective tenants can be done in ways similar to those used with prospective buyers: individual appointments, private open houses attended by multiple prospects whom you've invited, or public open houses where anyone who has seen your ad or knows of the vacancy can show up.

Of course, you probably won't have your real estate agent there to do the showings for you. You can either show the property yourself (not a bad idea, given that you'll be dealing with this person a lot in the months ahead), or hand the task over to a property manager if you hire one.

Screening Interested Tenants

Even if you find a tenant by word of mouth, don't just count yourself lucky and set a move-in date. Screening and choosing among prospective tenants is incredibly important—and hard to do based on gut instincts alone. A wrong choice can result in property damage and lost rent. And tenant turnover is always expensive. At worst, you could get stuck trying to figure out how to evict a deadbeat or troublesome tenant.

To avoid problems, ask each prospective tenant to fill out a rental application that includes:

- the applicant's employment, income, credit, and rental housing history
- up-to-date references from landlords and employers
- identifying information, such as Social Security number (SSN), driver's license number, passport, or Individual Taxpayer Identification Number (ITIN) which is issued by the IRS to persons who are required to file income taxes but who can't obtain a Social Security number, and
- details on past bankruptcies, evictions, or criminal convictions (you'll also get much of this information from a credit report, as discussed next).

But don't stop there. People who look good on paper may still be lying or covering up a negative rental or financial history. You'll want to choose your top two or three applicants and confirm what they've said on their applications. Call their previous landlords and other references for a summary of their character; call their employers to verify income and length of employment; and order a copy of each person's credit report.

To order credit reports, you'll need to work through a credit-reporting or tenant-screening service (type "tenant screening" or "credit report" into your browser's search box). It's legal in most states to charge prospective tenants a fee for the cost of the credit report and your time and trouble—$20 to $30 is common.

By following these steps, you should be able to find a high-quality tenant who will pay you the rent that you're counting on to maintain your house until the market is ripe for a sale.

How Renting Out Your House Affects Capital Gains Taxes

When real estate is eventually sold for an overall profit, the sellers may owe federal capital gains taxes. Fortunately, most sellers can take advantage of the standard exclusion, which shields $250,000 in individual profit and $500,000 in profit for a married couple filing jointly. But this exclusion comes with a critical requirement: You must be able to show that you both owned and lived in the house for two out of the last five years.

If you're planning to rent out your property for only a short time, perhaps while you're waiting for the market to turn around, this shouldn't present a problem. In fact, as long as you sell the house within three years of the day you stopped occupying it, you're still protected by the exclusion. But if the date of sale is even one day over that three-year period, you'll have lived in the house for less than two years out of the previous five and will have to pay capital gains taxes at whatever rate applies then.

Number one tax myth in the U.S.:

Three out of ten taxpayers mistakenly believe that they can write off losses from a home sale, according to a survey by CCH (www.cch.com).

⊘ **CAUTION**

Don't be confused by reports of 2008 changes to the capital gains tax laws for homes used as both residences and rental properties. The new laws apply only to homes that were *first* used as vacation or rental places and then converted to residences before being sold. (In those cases, the sellers must reduce pro rata the amount of profit they exclude based on the number of years the house was used as a rental.) You're in the reverse situation and, therefore, are still covered by the old laws.

Of course, if you break even or sell your house at a loss, you won't have to worry about capital gains taxes at all. For more information, see IRS Publication 523, *Selling Your Home*, available at www.irs.gov. ●

Seal the Deal:
Negotiating a Successful Sale

Meet Your Adviser

Joel G. Kinney, partner with Goldstein & Herndon, LLP, in Chestnut Hill, Massachusetts

What he does: Joel has handled both residential and commercial real estate legal matters in the greater Boston area for over seven years—long enough to have helped clients during both good and bad times in the real estate market. His practice covers a multitude of real estate, development, and zoning issues with respect to single-family homes, condominiums, and commercial developments.

Favorite money-saving strategy in tough times: "Pack your lunch for work! That's what I do—salami and cheese is my first choice. I probably save $50 a week that way. Also, getting a coffee machine for your office can save, I don't know, millions."

Likes best about his work: "When I get to work with clients and various professionals—mortgage brokers, real estate agents, lenders, and others—to create a successful deal for all involved."

Strangest thing he's seen sellers do:

"The worst was a case in which I was representing the buyer in a condominium sale, and he called me to ask for some information related to the closing. During our conversation, he happened to mention, 'I haven't finished the kitchen yet.' I had no idea what he meant. So he explained, 'The seller agreed that I could redo the kitchen before moving into the property.' I was stunned—they had negotiated this completely on the side, without considering any of the risks and liability issues. What if the transaction didn't close, and the seller wanted the buyer to undo the changes to the kitchen? Or what if the buyer had hit a gas line? Or damaged something in the condominium common areas?"

Top tip for homesellers:

"The more headaches you deal with earlier, the fewer you'll have later. For example, when you talk to your attorney—and I do advise hiring one, especially in this market—bring up any problems of which you are aware. These might be things like a septic system that won't pass inspection, boundary line disputes, easements, and an impending divorce or bankruptcy. Attorneys spend a lot of time picking up the pieces when something goes wrong in a transaction, but we can be even more useful recommending ways to avoid common problems in the first place."

Receiving an offer to buy your home is worth getting excited about. At last, your planning and preparation have paid off, and you can sleep without the deep-seated fear that no buyer will ever come along. You've almost reached your goal!

But don't start the party just yet. The final strategy in this book is to make sure the transaction goes smoothly, so you don't lose the deal after having come this far. We'll cover all the steps between initial offer and final sale, including:

- what form the buyer's offer might take and how to turn that into a legally binding, mutual agreement

- what makes a strong offer, in terms of price and other factors

- your responsibilities, and how to keep the buyer from backing out in the weeks before the closing, and

- what to expect on closing day.

What the Buyer's Offer Will Look Like

The real estate industry has developed established practices for how the buyer will submit an offer to you. Because these practices vary state by state, we can't tell you exactly what form the buyer's offer will take. Not to worry, your real estate agent will know the process very well. (And if you're selling FSBO, you can contact your state's department of real estate to get information on how things are handled.)

You'll most likely receive the offer in writing, probably a standard form created by your state's Realtor® association. These forms include not only the buyer's proposed price, but the conditions (contingencies) that must be met for the deal to finalize, the procedures for resolving any disputes between the buyer and you, who will pay what fees (such as for the escrow or title agent and other closing fees), and other details. In fact, in many states, the standard written offer is so comprehensive that you'd simply need to sign it (and in some states, have an attorney review it) for it to serve as a complete purchase contract. (Of course, you'd want to review the document carefully before doing this, because it's full of important terms you need to understand.)

In a few states, however, the standard offer is a very short document that simply communicates a wish to buy the house at a certain price. The buyer then waits for you, the seller, to create the first draft of the purchase agreement (with help from your real estate agent or attorney). In some states, these offers may even be oral, rather than written. That's okay, but only a written sales contract is valid, so at some point, you'll both have to sign on the dotted line.

Negotiating Strategy in a Tough Market

Negotiating over *anything* tends to be more relaxed in good economic times, when people are less focused on the bottom line. And unless your house or neighborhood happens to be hotter than average, a down market definitely puts you in the weaker negotiating position.

But does that mean you need to roll over and play dead or accede to the buyer's every demand? No, says adviser George Devine: "First off, no matter how desperate you feel, don't let people see you sweat—then they'll only ask for more. For example, I represented a couple where the wife was seven months pregnant and they had two other kids squeezed into a two-bedroom house. They really wanted to get out of there, but because I didn't want buyers to catch on to that fact, I made sure they never saw my client. (We're under no legal obligation to disclose the seller's personal situation.)"

It's best to project a calm and measured approach throughout the negotiations. Instead of rushing to answer a counteroffer, for instance, your agent might say, "We're going to need some time to think this over—can we get back to you in 24 hours?" George Devine adds, "It doesn't hurt to let the buyer sit and stew for a little while."

As for the details of what you'll say yes and no to, that depends to some degree on how eager you are to sell. Adviser Nancy Atwood says, "I like to try to devise a win-win strategy. For example, if the buyer is pushing for a new heating system AND a new roof, then we might negotiate one or the other, plus offer a concession towards costs."

To present the offer, the buyer's agent will likely get in touch with your agent and arrange to meet and discuss the offer in person. You'll probably want to come to this meeting, but it's unlikely that the buyers themselves will attend. If you receive more than one offer around the same time, you can ask that they be presented on the same day.

How soon do you need to respond? Check the offer itself, which should specify a date and time when it will automatically expire. Some buyers put short expiration dates on their offers, to push you into action. In dismal market conditions, this will probably force you to respond quickly (with an acceptance or at least a counteroffer) unless you decide to simply reject it in hopes of getting another, better offer later.

Back and Forth: From Offer to Contract

After the buyer has submitted an offer, you can respond in one of three ways:

- Accept the offer.
- Reject the offer.
- Make a counteroffer.

> **TIP**
>
> **The first offer is often the best.** "I always tell my clients to look very hard at the first offer they receive," says Tampa Bay Realtor® Rick Woods. "Of course, if a long time passes before the next offer comes in, that one is likely to be for a lower amount."

Accepting the Offer

If the buyer's offer is already in the form of the proposed contract, you're happy with the price, the buyer's finances line up, and everything in it looks good, with no need for additions or alterations, you don't have much more to do. (This doesn't happen very often!) You'd need only to sign the offer document and return it to the buyer, and you would have a contract binding both of you (subject to getting it reviewed by an attorney, if that's required in your state).

> **CAUTION**
>
> **You may have to accept an offer—but only if it's perfect.** In some states, if a buyer comes in with a totally clean, no-contingency, full-price offer, you're obligated to either sell to that person or take the house off the market.

If the buyer's offer is only a brief document or an oral offer, and you want to accept it, you can let the buyer know, then figure out the logistics of drafting a contract (most likely, through either your agents or attorneys working together). You and the buyer will then negotiate over the contract until you've got it into a form that both of you are happy to sign.

Until that contract is signed, however, neither of you is bound by the agreement, and that means either one of you could walk away. For that reason, some buyers ask for what's called a binder, which is a preliminary agreement secured by the buyer's payment of earnest money (usually a nominal amount). You might think of it as a contract to negotiate a contract. Binders can be helpful for situations where, for instance, the attorneys can't get together right away, and the buyer wants assurances that another buyer won't step in. However, for ordinary situations, many attorneys counsel against binders. Richard Leshnower, an attorney in New York, explains: "A binder is often more trouble than it's worth. Because it's not a full purchase contract, there are a lot of terms it doesn't have, and you can end up with messy and expensive litigation between two parties who are, realistically, never going to agree to the sale." It's probably simpler and more straightforward to focus your energies on getting an agreement on paper with which both you and the buyer are comfortable.

Rejecting the Offer

Maybe you can already tell—perhaps by an absurdly low price or an unrealistic contingency—that the buyer's offer will do nothing but waste your time and delay your eventual sale if you accept it and take your house off the market. If so, your agent can contact the buyer's agent with the bad news.

Have the courtesy to respond. Some sellers do nothing when they receive an offer they don't plan to accept or negotiate. Better to have your agent make the call, and even briefly describe the problem ("The offer was so far below the asking price that we really didn't think it would be possible to find a middle ground"). The buyers may even respond by correcting the problem.

If no other offers are on the table, however, think twice before saying no. As adviser Jaan Henry says, "I almost never reject any offer outright—you can miss a lot of opportunities that way." The counteroffer process gives you an opportunity to test whether the buyer has really made the best offer he or she is capable of.

Making a Counteroffer

There are so many different terms in an offer that it's rare to find one that meets your criteria in every respect. If the offer looks promising, but you'd prefer a few changes or additions, you can make a counteroffer—even in a down market. Counteroffers are a normal part of nearly every real estate deal. For example, you might suggest a higher price than was offered (but probably lower than your list price, if you want your negotiations to go anywhere). Or you might add terms of your own, for example by responding to a tight closing date with a clause allowing you to rent back the house for a couple of weeks.

A wise counteroffer in the current market, according to adviser Joel G. Kinney, is to ask for "dollar limits on paying for repair needs that come up after the inspection, particularly if you're accepting a lower-than-list price. For example, a seller who lists a house for $350,000, but decides to accept $320,000, probably doesn't want to be nickeled and dimed over repairs. That seller might limit repair costs to, say, $5,000 or $6,000." (In some states, such a limit is written into the standard contract, although you're free to change the amount. Florida, for example, sets a default limit of 1½% of the sales price.)

The form of your counteroffer depends on local custom and what form the original offer took. If the original offer would have worked as a standalone contract, you might start from scratch and fill out a whole new version of the exact same form. Or you might create a simpler document, essentially saying, "I agree to the terms of the offer, but with these changes." Or, simpler still, you and your agent might suggest a counteroffer verbally during your initial meeting with the buyer's agent, and the buyer's agent might call the buyer to discuss the matter before the final step, when it all gets put into writing (and only then becomes legally binding).

If your counteroffer terms are acceptable, the buyer may either sign on and create a contract or submit further counteroffers. This process may go back and forth until you've come to an agreement that either is or can be formalized in a written document.

Arranging for Backup Offers

If you're lucky enough to receive more than one strong offer, you have a tough choice: Which do you choose? And what if the one you choose ends up falling through?

One possible way to protect yourself is to ask your second-choice offeror to leave the offer open, as a "backup offer." If the chosen deal falls apart, you can then accept the backup. Or, if the first offeror is asking for a lot of concessions, you can use the backup offer as negotiating leverage. Unfortunately, the buyer in the backup position can withdraw the offer at any time and may also condition his or her backup position on your giving a final acceptance or rejection within a limited time, perhaps only a few days. On top of that, if your first-choice buyer knows about the backup deal (information that the agents might share), he or she may feel like you're playing the field a bit too much, making for a rocky start to your relationship.

A less formal, but often more effective approach is described by adviser Mark Nash: "I sometimes call the agent for our second-choice buyer and say, 'We appreciate your offer, but we have another offer that we believe will move forward. If anything happens, however, we'll contact you.' That serves to keep the house in the minds of the alternate buyers and their agent."

Signing the Purchase Contract

Once you've agreed on the terms of your sale, there's one last important step: signing off on the document that becomes your purchase agreement. By now, one of you has probably either created an offer or counteroffer that will serve as a final contract, or you've come to a close enough agreement that it will be easy for either your real estate agent or attorney to put it in written form. Give the contract one last read-through, to make sure you understand all the terms to which you're agreeing.

Then you (and any co-owners) simply sign and date the latest version. The buyers will need to sign, too, if they haven't already. Or, if they've already signed but you've mutually agreed to certain changes, they may need to initial the changes. The buyer's real estate agent may also sign, essentially as a witness to the buyer's signature.

Only then, when you have a written document, signed by both you and the buyer, are you legally bound by your agreement.

Serious Buyer or Lowballer? Evaluating the Financial Parts of the Offer

The envelope please: You're probably dying to see what price your prospective buyer has offered. But that's not all you should look at. There's lots of other financial information within the typical offer, which will help you decide whether the buyer is really ready and able to close a sale.

In fact, if you're lucky enough to receive multiple offers, you won't necessarily want to choose the highest-priced one. A buyer with solid financial backing—or even better, who's offering all cash—may be your best bet, even at a lower price.

Price

If you're offered your asking price, let out a cheer. But more likely, your buyers will figure they've got a good shot at getting the house for less, particularly if it's been on the market for a while.

> ⓘ **CAUTION**
> **No matter the price, every offer has to pass the appraisal test.** As adviser Mark Nash explains, "Even if you find a buyer willing to pay a little more than market price, the lender could refuse to finance the loan where the sales price is higher than the property's appraised value." For more on this issue, see "Getting Past the Appraisal," below.

The question is, how much less than your asking price should you accept? If the proposed amount is at the lower end of what you'd expected or hoped to get, and no other offers seem to be on the horizon, it's definitely worth considering. Waiting for a higher offer will risk the house going stale on the market and will add to your costs—especially if you've already moved out and have to keep paying utilities on your empty house and rental fees on any furniture. And of course, there's no guarantee that a better offer will come along.

If the offered price is even lower than that, you've got some thinking to do. While you may be tempted to decline outright or to counteroffer much closer to your asking price, do some objective evaluation first. Consider what the general interest level in your house has been so far, taking into account issues like:

- **How many times have brokers shown your home to their clients?** If buyers aren't coming by—either because they're not interested or their brokers are taking them elsewhere—it could mean you're fortunate to have an offer at all.

- **What level of interest have visitors shown?** If you've seen excitement and follow-up questions or even previous offers that didn't work out or were too low, you may want to wait. But if you've heard nothing or vague promises to "think about it," that low offer may start to look good.

- **How long has the house been on the market?** The longer it's been available, the more likely you'll have to compromise on price. (See Chapter 8 for tips on when to actually publish a lower list price.)

- **Were you planning on a similar price drop anyway?** If you were considering slashing your price to a point at or near the offer amount at some point anyway, you might accept the offer you have now, or at least counter it.

- **Can you afford to wait?** Are you getting seriously strapped for cash that you're counting on to buy another house? If so, it may be time to take the offer and cut your losses, if you can afford to.

- **What's it costing you?** If you've already moved and are making two mortgage payments, is it worth continuing to do so in hopes of getting a much better offer in the relatively short term? Also add in how much it costs to keep the house looking good for visitors.

- **What are the latest sold comparables showing?** Prices may have dropped even in the last few weeks, and as discussed further below, you'll probably have to get your price past an appraiser for the buyer's lender in order to close the sale, so a lower price may be your only choice for making the deal work.

Taking into account these market realities, try to judge just how realistic and fair a buyer's offer is. It can feel annoying, and even insulting, to see someone trying to turn your home into a bargain—especially when you're hoping to sell for as much as possible. But with lots of homes available in the market, practically every buyer starts to have visions of getting an amazing deal. Try to focus on meeting your goal—selling your home for its current market value—instead of fixating on whether you're getting everything you want.

Earnest-Money Deposit

The offer may be accompanied by a sum of money called an earnest-money or good-faith deposit. (In fact, you may have specified an earnest-money requirement in your listing and set the required amount, most likely at a certain percentage of the purchase price.) Sometimes the deposit is paid in two parts: a flat fee (typically $500 or $1,000) when the offer is submitted, and the rest, usually a percentage of the purchase price, when the contract is signed. The idea is that a buyer who backs out of the deal for a reason not contemplated in the contract will forfeit this sum. A buyer who goes through with the deal can either get a refund of the earnest-money deposit or apply the money toward closing costs.

If you didn't specify a requested amount, the buyer will make a choice depending on local custom (within any limits set by state law) and how badly the buyer wants the house. A high deposit indicates a high level of commitment to the deal. Of course, in a down market, buyers are less likely to feel the type of urgency that might drive them to go extra high on the earnest-money amount. They know it's not likely to sway you and figure there's no point in putting more cash on the line than necessary.

Down Payment Amount

The offer should state how much the buyer plans to pay in cash toward the purchase price. Ideally, this amount is 20% or more. Anything less than 5% makes the transaction questionable, because the buyer will have a hard time finding a reputable institution to lend the rest.

Also look at when exactly the buyer plans to make the down payment. For example, the buyer may suggest putting down 10% within the first two weeks of signing the purchase agreement and the remaining 10% at closing. Adviser and broker Jaan Henry notes, "In your counteroffer, you can ask the buyer to make a larger down payment up-front, as evidence of the buyer's ability to perform."

Financing Contingency

Almost as important as the offer amount is how the buyer plans to pull the rest of the money together, and the chances of getting a bank loan for that amount. Brace yourself—this is seriously important to your deal going through, so we're going to spill a lot of ink about it.

Unless you receive an all-cash offer (unlikely), the buyer will probably include a financing contingency in the offer. This states that the agreement will be finalized only if the buyer applies for financing within a certain time period and then successfully obtains a loan on certain specified terms. (For example, buyers might state within the offer that they'll accept only a fixed-rate loan at 6% interest or less—although not all offers are written to include this level of detail.) Let's look closer at how you should evaluate the financing contingency.

Is the Buyer Preapproved?

Your first question should be about what efforts the buyer has already made to obtain financing. A prepared buyer will have already gotten loan preapproval; that is, a lender's statement of willingness to lend a certain amount of cash. With preapproval for an amount equal to or greater than the sale price of your home, a buyer should be able to get the loan when the time comes. Such preapproval is more important in the current market than ever, with lenders doing massive amounts of investigating and double-checking before giving actual, final approval to a loan—or denying it.

> **CAUTION**
>
> **Even a preapproval isn't necessarily a commitment.** As adviser Joel G. Kinney explains, "Sellers need to be aware of the difference. The most solid preapprovals are ones where the lender went over the buyer's finances before preapproving, which is more likely to happen at established, reputable lending institutions rather than the local discount loan house. Your real estate agent or attorney can help you evaluate which are the reputable lenders."

If the buyer hasn't been preapproved for a loan at all (and shown you a letter to prove it), your deal may be an iffy proposition. In the best-case scenario, the buyer may have started house shopping only recently, without realizing the need for loan preapproval. In the worst-case scenario, the buyer has bad credit and hasn't yet found a willing lender, but is hoping for a change of luck. In either case, take a look at the loan terms the buyer is hoping to get—if those seem completely out of whack in today's market, that's a strike against this offer. Also consider the buyer's down payment— the bigger it is, the more likely the buyer will get the needed financing, because the buyer's bigger investment lowers the lender's risk.

If you're inclined to continue with the negotiations, insist that a buyer who doesn't have loan preapproval get one from an established lender before you agree to the financing contingency—and ask your agent to call the lender and confirm the preapproval letter's authenticity. Also have any prospective buyer provide additional financial information, discussed further below.

Selling a Condo? Make Sure Lenders Won't Refuse to Touch It

If you're selling a condo, the buyers' eligibility isn't the lender's only concern. Under 2008 Fannie Mae/Freddie Mac guidelines, lenders must, before approving a condo loan, evaluate things like the condo association's financial stability, what ratio of the property is occupied by renters, how much space is reserved for certain usages, and more.

Not surprisingly, this has made it more difficult for buyers to take out loans for a condo purchase. Adviser Joel G. Kinney notes, "In a market like Boston, where many homes have been converted to condos, the property may simply not fit the guidelines. One way sellers can deal with such potential problems is to get the property preapproved by a lender. In literal terms, you'd go to a mortgage broker and say, 'Can you find an investor that will loan on this condo?'

"Once you have that preapproval, you can tell buyers that the condo has passed at least one lender's examination review and it fits within the lending guidelines. (Any loan would of course have to go through the underwriting process, but good loan officers will be able to tell with some assurance whether or not a condo project can be funded.) You could even put a contingency into your purchase contract saying that the buyer must submit a loan application to that particular lender (among others, if the buyer wishes)."

Set an Appropriate Schedule for Financing

Another issue to consider is when, in the weeks before the proposed deal would close, you'll find out about the likelihood that the financing will come through. As Joel G. Kinney explains, "The standard purchase contract mentions the date by which the lender must issue an actual loan commitment letter, which will itself contain certain conditions before final approval—perhaps verification of the buyer's employment or the need for a professional appraisal of the house's value. Make sure the date for this commitment letter isn't so far out that the buyer can withdraw from the transaction right before closing. For example, if the closing is scheduled for November 28, and the mortgage contingency date isn't until November 24, what happens if the buyer doesn't get the commitment and it's four days before closing? Your sale could fall apart at the last minute." At the least, you'll want to negotiate for a date that lets you know sooner rather than later whether the financing will come through.

Get Additional Financial Information From the Buyer

In today's tight credit market with many people facing financial troubles that make them less creditworthy, you want as much financial information as possible from a potential buyer. For this reason, you may want to ask for additional documentation, to see for yourself whether the buyer is in a good position to get a mortgage loan.

Adviser Jaan Henry says, "I send a questionnaire to the buyer's agent asking that the buyer, loan rep, and whoever is involved fill it out. Very few selling agents request this much information, but I consider it important for evaluating the offer, particularly as regards the buyer's ability to follow through financially. Obviously I can't compel the buyer to respond, but I explain that the seller will make a determination about the offer based on the information at hand." In a down market, a picky buyer may refuse if he or she thinks it's too big a hassle. But as Henry says, there's no harm in asking for the following:

- **Full contact information for the buyer, the buyer's agent, and the attorney (if any).** "This helps in case the information provided in the offer is incomplete."

- **Status of mortgage approval.** "If an application is underway, we ask for the name and contact information for the lender and mortgage officer."

- **The offer and down payment amounts.** "We ask that this include an explanation of where the down payment funds will come from (cash on hand, pension, money market, gifts, proceeds from another sale, etc.) and the dollar amounts for each category."

- **Whether the buyer is selling another property before buying this one.** "If so, we ask what stage the sale is at, and whether the buyer will be relying on those funds to buy this house."

- **FICO credit scores for each buyer.** "We ask for all three scores, from each of the major credit reporting agencies. Even for a full-price offer, if the FICO scores aren't at 700 or above, we'll probably end up rejecting the offer. That's the threshold among lenders today—it used to be 650 was the bottom line, but now it's tougher."

- **The buyer's credit ratios.** "We ask for both the front- and back-end percentages (mortgage and total debt versus income, discussed in greater detail in Chapter 5) and compare that with what a lender is likely to approve. A bank will look particularly hard at the buyer's 'debt-to-income ratio,' which should ideally be about 36% or less. That is, all debts, including mortgage debt, should eat up only about 36% of the buyer's gross income."

- **Whether the buyer is self-employed.** "If so, we ask what kind of business the buyer runs and for how long it's been in operation. Again, this helps us predict the likelihood of the buyer getting a loan on the necessary terms."

Talk with your agent about possibly asking prospective buyers for some or all of this information.

Big-Deal Details: Other Important Contract Terms

In the course of preparing the final contract, you and the buyer will have to work out various other terms of the deal. Here are the most important ones.

Closing Date

The closing date is when the transaction finalizes and the house is legally transferred from you to the buyer. Typically, the contract will specify an actual closing date, around 30 to 90 days into the future. In some states, however, standard contracts give a certain time window or say "on or before" or "on or after" a certain date.

Some buyers (who will be doing most of the work in the days leading up to the closing and may have to sell their own home first) won't want to feel rushed into the purchase. In that case, they'll have little interest in setting a tight deadline. Your interests are to some extent the opposite. Of course, you want to allow enough time for you and the buyer to do things right and for you to move out (if you haven't already).

Still, the last thing you want is for the buyer to take a leisurely period of months inspecting every corner of the house and otherwise preparing for the closing. That could not only delay your ability to get your money out of the house, but also risk running the buyer's financing—there may be an expiration date on the lender's loan commitment or interest rate lock. So try to limit the closing date to no more than 60 days after the contract signing. And whatever you do, don't agree to close within a "reasonable time." What's reasonable to you may not be what's reasonable to the buyer. Far better to set a date, which you and the buyer can later agree (in writing) to change if you need to.

The contract may also state a separate date of possession. That's the day when the buyer can move into the property. Normally, this is the same date as the closing date, but you can agree on a different date.

Home Sale Contingency

A buyer who plans to sell another house before buying yours probably won't have any available cash until that sale happens. Such buyers may want a contingency in the purchase contract stating that the deal is conditional upon their selling their house. Without such a contingency, the buyer could get stuck owing you for the house, without having the means to pay for it.

Still, you're not going to be happy to see this contingency. If you're having trouble selling your own home, who knows how much trouble the buyer will have? (The contingency may be a bit more palatable if the buyer's home is in an area where home sales are happening at a steady pace.)

In any case, if you're looking at your only reasonable offer, or the only one likely to arrive soon, you may want to agree to the contingency. But you can create a compromise that protects you: Negotiate to have the contract include a "wipeout" clause, which lets you leave your house on the market while you wait for the buyer to sell. If you get another offer, you'll advise the buyer, in essence, "You have xx hours (usually 72) to either wipe out the contingency and continue with the purchase or free me from the contract so I can sell to the other offeror."

If, after invoking the wipeout clause, the buyer can't go forward with buying your house, the contract will be canceled. You'll have to return the earnest-money deposit, too. At that point, you'll be free to continue negotiations with the new offeror.

Inspection Contingency

You can expect that the buyer will want to include an inspection contingency. This clause gives the buyer a chance to inspect your house and to either approve the results or negotiate over needed repairs, as a condition of closing the deal. Although this obviously leaves a giant window of opportunity for buyers who get cold feet and want to cancel the contract, that's no reason to argue over a contingency that is standard and reasonable.

Title Report Contingency

The buyer will also want the right to hire a title officer or attorney to review the history of your house's ownership. The basic idea of the title report contingency is to make sure that you truly own the house outright, without any outstanding debts against it that won't be resolved when the transaction closes. This, too, is a reasonable term to put in the offer and contract.

Homeowners' Insurance Contingency

The buyer may wish to condition the sale on successfully obtaining hazard insurance coverage for your house. This probably isn't a contingency to fight about.

Attorney Review Contingency

Either the buyer or you may wish to put a clause in your final contract making the deal contingent on your attorney reviewing it and your being satisfied with the results. (In fact, such attorney review is required in some states.) You'd still sign the contract, but the attorney may suggest amendments after the fact. This can be especially important if you're selling without an agent.

Contingency for Review of CC&Rs or Other Documents

If you're selling a condominium or other property in a common interest development, your buyer will no doubt request the right to review the CC&Rs, master deed, bylaws, rules and regulations, and other relevant documents before agreeing to the sale. These will tell the buyer important things like how well funded and well run the governing association is, what the community rules are, and how much to expect to pay in fees and special assessments.

It's only fair to agree to this. Any homebuyer who has read the headlines lately knows to be cautious about buying a condominium in the current economic environment. In developments where a number of units are unsold, vacant, or being foreclosed on, the remaining owners and new buyers often have to pay extra-high fees just to keep the condo association afloat and able to maintain the property.

Who Pays Which Fees

In Chapter 6, we discussed creating incentives by offering to pay some of the fees normally paid by the buyer. The buyer may ask for you to pay some fees (such as escrow fees, title search fees, deed preparation fees, notary fees, and transfer taxes), even if you haven't already volunteered to do so, by checking off boxes on a standard offer form or through some other written notation.

Even if you hadn't originally planned on paying these costs, they make a nice incentive for the buyer, and you might use them to compensate for some other part of your counteroffer that the buyer will be less happy about—for example, a rent-back period or a shorter escrow period. Some buyers will even pay a slightly higher price than offered, for the convenience of having extra cash at the closing table.

Between Signing and Closing: Escrow

Once escrow begins, many people will spring into action: The escrow or title agent named in your contract will start ordering or preparing title reports, preparing the property deed, and more; the buyer's lender will begin in-depth review and processing of the loan and order a professional appraisal of your home; and the buyer will arrange for pest and general inspections and homeowners' insurance, plus work on meeting any other contingencies.

Thankfully, your responsibilities during this time period are relatively few. Your most important tasks will include making your home available when needed for inspections and appraisals, preparing various forms and statements (such as disclosures if you haven't already prepared these, and any other forms required locally, such as a smoke detector certificate), and meeting any other contingencies you agreed to in your contract, within the promised time frame (for example, getting copies of permits for work you did on your kitchen).

More generally, you'll need to be available and responsive when issues arise. For example, if the title search turns up a lien on your property placed by a contractor who claims you didn't pay the bill, you'll need to deal with this to clear the property's title. If the inspection report turns up repair needs, you'll have to decide how to respond to the buyer's requests, which might include consulting contractors or making actual repairs. Meanwhile, you'll be busy planning your move to your next abode, if you haven't already moved.

Plan on staying in close touch with your real estate and escrow agents during this time, to make sure you stay on track. There's enough risk of the buyer having a change of mind without your making matters worse by missing a deadline or forgetting to respond to a request.

Getting Past the Appraisal

Even if you've found a buyer willing to purchase your house for a price you're willing to sell for, it's not only the buyer who must agree. Except in the rare cases when a buyer is paying cash for your home, it's likely that the buyer's mortgage lender will require that the property be appraised—that is, that a professional, selected by the lender, will come to the property and look around, then put a dollar figure on its value.

It used to be that appraisals were little more than formalities, which lenders required to ensure that buyers weren't purchasing tear-down trash heaps. But not so today, with lenders edgy after losing money to defaulting homeowners and getting stuck with properties worth less than the mortgages held against them. As adviser Mark Nash explains, "We're really not in a world where the buyer and seller set the price anymore. Remember that the lender is carrying the risk, and their appraiser has the final say, most likely based on recent prices of comparable sales."

Because you've done your market research, odds are that your price is perfectly appropriate. But just be aware that surprises can happen, especially if market conditions have changed in the last few weeks. And you can't do much to control the appraiser's judgment of your house's value, since it's based on objective factors like the price of what's sold recently. (Of course, it doesn't hurt to make sure the house looks good and that you've resolved any obvious repair or safety issues before the appraiser comes over and looks around.)

If the appraisal comes in lower than the contract price, the bank will not approve the buyer's loan, and if there's a financing contingency, that will probably kill the deal. The buyer may dispute the appraisal value with the bank, in hopes of getting the loan anyway, or come up with the extra cash. Alternatively, the buyer may look elsewhere for a loan, though it's unlikely you'll find another lender's appraiser to say something significantly different. Absent that, you're going to have to decide whether to accept a lower price— likely, the appraised value, which is the maximum the lender will allow the buyer to pay, and in all likelihood, the maximum the buyer will be *willing* to pay, after hearing a professional's take on what the house is really worth.

Dealing With the Inspection Contingency

One of the biggest hurdles to clear is the inspection contingency. Hopefully, your own advance inspection of the property has ruled out major problems that can't be fixed (such as pervasive mold) or ones that significantly reduce the property's value (such as foundation or roof trouble, or remodeling that wasn't up to code). But even if you did your own inspection, your house is practically guaranteed to have a few defects. As adviser Nancy Atwood says, "All homes (except new construction) have issues that we refer to as the 'price of homeownership:' loose tiles, old paint, and so forth." And the buyer's inspector wouldn't be doing the job right without noting everything in the report from a missing cover plate on an electrical outlet to a crack in the foundation.

Your contract probably gives the buyer a certain number of days (such as three) within which to "approve" or "disapprove" of the report. It doesn't really matter how bad the problems are—the buyer now has an opportunity to say, "Forget it," and end the deal.

Assuming the buyer doesn't cut and run, the most likely thing to happen within the approval period is that the buyer will negotiate over the needed repairs—possibly every little repair, if the buyer is truly inclined to take advantage of your weak position in the down market. Procedurally speaking, the buyer may ask for any of the following:

- **An escrow credit.** Instead of getting the full price at closing, you can instead agree to have the amount needed for repairs transferred directly to the buyer at closing or put into an escrow account (maintained by your escrow or title agent), which the buyer can draw on anytime after the closing. (Lenders prefer the latter approach, because it gives the buyer an incentive to actually make the repairs; in fact, a very stringent lender won't fund the loan until the repairs are made, thus delaying the closing.) To set an appropriate amount for the credit, you'll probably get actual contractor bids.

- **A reduction in the sale price.** If your house is worth less than originally thought as a result of the defects, you can also just lower the price to reflect that. This lowers any required transfer taxes (for whoever has to pay them) and the buyer's annual property tax. Of course, figuring out how much to lower the price by is tricky—again, you might want to get bids for repairs.

- **Repairs to be made by you.** It's unlikely, but possible, that the buyer will ask you to make repairs. (Most buyers prefer to be in charge of overseeing repairs themselves.) While you have to come up with cash if the buyer requests this, at least you'll be able to choose the contractor and have some control over the price—or if it's a simple fix-up, even take care of it yourself.

- **Repairs to be arranged by the buyer before closing, with you paying the bill.** This should be the buyer's last choice—and yours as well. It requires three-way coordination between you, the buyer, and the buyer's repair people while you're still living in the house, as well as dealing with the possibility that the repairs will take longer than expected.

You can either agree to the price or repair requests outright, suggest minor changes, or refuse some requests. But think twice before refusing: In a down market, buyers know they're in the better bargaining position and can probably find another, more pliable seller.

Dealing With the Title Contingency

If any clouds on your house title are discovered, you'll need to deal with them quickly—which can sometimes mean coming up with some immediate cash. For example, if there's a lien on your house for unpaid child support, it's probably not going to be removed until you pay the child support.

Preparing for the Final Walk-Through

Another, often overlooked contingency that's probably in your contract is the final walk-through. This allows the buyer and buyer's agent, as one of the last steps during the days or hours before the closing, to visit your house and make sure that you've left it in the agreed-upon physical condition. You'll need to have moved out of the house (unless otherwise agreed), made any negotiated repairs, left behind all fixtures and other agreed-upon property, moved out all of your own things, and left the place clean.

If you fail in one of your responsibilities, the buyer can use this as an excuse to delay the closing, bring up new repair or price requests (possibly getting a last-minute credit in escrow to make sure you take care of matters), or even cancel the sale. Adviser Joel G. Kinney remembers, "I represented a buyer in a house sale where, at the final walk-through, the buyer discovered that the seller had taken all the cabinet hardware off. When we brought it up, the seller said, 'I bought these, they're special handles, and I'm taking them with me.' That doesn't work—cabinet handles are fixtures, and the seller should have either swapped them out before showing the house or negotiated their removal as part of the purchase agreement. We made him put them all back."

A lot of sellers fall down on the job when it comes to final cleanup. You may be madly packing and moving into a new house yourself, and it's easy to forget a few boxes or a pile of trash in your old place. But wouldn't you be kicking yourself if the buyer made an issue of this?

Take careful note of the final walk-through date, and make plans to have your house empty and spotless before that time. Do your own final walk-through, looking out for any repair issues that were previously hidden by your possessions. If, for example, some missing paint or plaster was hidden behind a bookshelf, or was created by your moving crew, do a quick touch up. If you haven't been living in the house, make sure no new damage has occurred while you've been away, such as leaks or vandalism. Those too are your responsibility to fix before the closing.

If you're going to be too exhausted for major scrubbing, arrange for a cleaning service to come in after you. You're expected to at least leave the place "broom clean."

The Big Day: Your House Closing

Your wait is almost over. Here's what to expect on the closing day itself, when you'll exchange the buyer's money for your house. Whether you and the buyer meet face to face or conduct each of your halves of the transaction separately, the escrow agent will make sure that both of you feel safe handing over what you own to the other.

You'll most likely have a "closing meeting" in the office of either your escrow agent, attorney, or registry of deeds. The choice of location depends mostly on local custom and who will be present. In most cases, your agent will be there, as well as the escrow agent, if there is one, and possibly your attorney, if you're represented. If you're meeting face to face with the buyer, his or her agent will also be there, and possibly the buyer's attorney.

TIP

What if an emergency comes up and you or a co-owner can't be at the closing? It's possible to arrange to sign everything a few days beforehand, for example if you're traveling. Another possibility is to prepare a document called a "power of attorney," giving signing power to a trusted friend, relative, or lawyer. The power of attorney should include an expiration date—perhaps a few days after the closing. Check with your attorney or closing agent for details of how the power of attorney needs to be formatted and possibly recorded with a government office.

The closing is another occasion at which you'll have to remind yourself that you can't control everything. A lot has to come together for a closing to happen, and it's almost inevitable that something will go wrong, whether big or small. Fortunately, you'll be surrounded by a team of professionals, who've learned to deal with even the most difficult snafus. And by now, adviser Jaan Henry says, "The buyers must truly want the house. They've spent money on a home inspection, appraisal, and mortgage, and aren't likely to walk away from all that."

One of the biggest sources of closing snags is the buyer's lender, which must give its final agreement to the loan. No matter how much investigating the lender has done in the weeks leading up to the closing, it's not uncommon for lenders to raise last-minute issues or make demands, such as for reconfirmation of employment. Just rest assured that a delayed closing doesn't necessarily mean the deal falls apart—it usually just means you're in suspense for a little longer.

When the deal is finally done, celebrate! You've pulled off what many would-be sellers have been unable to do in this market and educated yourself so as to do it in the smartest way possible. Time to move on and start enjoying living in your next home.

Checklist of Items to Bring to the Closing

Make sure you've got all of the below ready to go:

- ❑ **Passport, driver's license, or other photo identification.** You may need to show it to the notary public who stamps the property deed or documents after you sign them.
- ❑ **Keys to your house.** The buyer will have trouble getting in without them!
- ❑ **Garage door opener.** Same issue.
- ❑ **House deed.** This will need to be turned over to the buyer, to transfer title. Your real estate agent will probably make sure this is taken care of, but talk to your escrow officer about whose responsibility it is if you're selling FSBO.
- ❑ **Home ownership records.** Closing is usually the most logical time to hand over your product and appliance manuals and warranties, records of recent repairs, and names of repair people you've used and liked.
- ❑ **Utility payment records.** In most cases, this means bringing receipts showing that you've paid the most recent water and sewer bills (which, if unpaid, can create liens on the property).
- ❑ **Any other required documents.** Your purchase contract may require you to deliver certain other items, such as condominium documents.

TIP

Want to leave a parting gift for your buyers? Adviser Jaan Henry says, "Some sellers leave a fruit basket, flowers, garden tools, or some other little gift, as a courtesy. It's not because I suggested it, but often because they had a wonderful time living in that house and want to pass on the good energy. Some also leave a note for the buyers, with any last bits of advice about vendors, repair people, or the name of the paper delivery person."

Documents to Keep From Your Sale

The homebuyer will be the one to walk away with most of the paperwork from your sale. Nevertheless, for future reference (especially on the off chance that the buyer later tries to raise any legal claims), it's worth keeping a file of your house-sale-related documents. These should include:

- ❏ **Your purchase contract.** This will remind you of everything you and the buyer agreed to.

- ❏ **Bill of sale (if any).** This will remind you of any personal property the buyer agreed to pay extra for, such as a children's swing set, curtains, or a floor rug.

- ❏ **Deed (or warranty deed).** You'll get a copy of the deed that you signed, telling the world that you've transferred the property to the buyer. The closing agent will, as the last step in closing on the property, file a copy with the appropriate public records office.

- ❏ **Affidavit of title and ALTA statement.** These are copies of documents you sign and give to the buyer swearing that you've done nothing to cloud the house's title and know of no unrecorded contracts, easements, or leases held against the property. These statements help finalize the buyer's request for title insurance.

- ❏ **Copy of RESPA/HUD-1 statement.** Also called the closing statement or settlement sheet, this is prepared by the title or closing agent. It gives a final accounting of all the various costs and fees that you and the buyer have paid or soon will pay to bring about the closing. You'll hopefully have already reviewed this statement for errors (you're supposed to get a good-faith estimate of these expenses within three days of applying for the loan and a draft of the final document at least a day in advance, under federal law). You'll need to sign the statement, as will the buyer and the closing agent.

- ❏ **Transfer tax documentation.** If you were required to pay a property transfer tax (which may be either a percentage of the sales price or a flat fee), you'll receive proof of payment.

- ❏ **Proration documents.** These show how you and the buyer are splitting up various costs for the month in which the house is being sold. If, for example, you've already paid this year's property taxes, the buyer will need to reimburse you for the portion of the tax bill covering the time of the buyer's ownership.

Index

Get the Latest in the Law

 Nolo's Legal Updater
We'll send you an email whenever a new edition of your book is published! Sign up at **www.nolo.com/legalupdater**.

 Updates at Nolo.com
Check **www.nolo.com/update** to find recent changes in the law that affect the current edition of your book.

 Nolo Customer Service
To make sure that this edition of the book is the most recent one, call us at **800-728-3555** and ask one of our friendly customer service representatives (7:00 am to 6:00 pm PST, weekdays only). Or find out at **www.nolo.com**.

 Complete the Registration & Comment Card...
...and we'll do the work for you! Just indicate your preferences below:

Registration & Comment Card

NAME _____ DATE _____

ADDRESS _____

CITY _____ STATE _____ ZIP _____

PHONE _____ EMAIL _____

COMMENTS _____

WAS THIS BOOK EASY TO USE?   (VERY EASY)   5   4   3   2   1   (VERY DIFFICULT)

☐ Yes, you can quote me in future Nolo promotional materials. *Please include phone number above.*

☐ Yes, send me **Nolo's Legal Updater** via email when a new edition of this book is available.

Yes, I want to sign up for the following email newsletters:

  ☐ **NoloBriefs** (monthly)
  ☐ **Nolo's Special Offer** (monthly)
  ☐ **Nolo's BizBriefs** (monthly)
  ☐ **Every Landlord's Quarterly** (four times a year)

☐ Yes, you can give my contact info to carefully selected partners whose products may be of interest to me.

DOWN1

Send to: **Nolo** 950 Parker Street Berkeley, CA 94710-9867, Fax: (800) 645-0895, or include all of the above information in an email to regcard@nolo.com with the subject line "DOWN1."

NOLO *and* USA TODAY

Cutting-Edge Content, Unparalleled Expertise

The Busy Family's Guide to Money

by Sandra Block, Kathy Chu & John Waggoner • $19.99

The Busy Family's Guide to Money will help you make the most of your income, handle major one-time expenses, figure children into the budget—and much more.

The Work From Home Handbook

Flex Your Time, Improve Your Life

by Diana Fitzpatrick & Stephen Fishman • $19.99

If you're one of those people who need to (or simply want to) work from home, let this book help you come up with a plan that both you and your boss can embrace!

Retire Happy

What You Can Do NOW to Guarantee a Great Retirement

by Richard Stim & Ralph Warner • $19.99

You don't need a million dollars to retire well, but you do need friends, hobbies and an active lifestyle. This book shows how to make retirement the best time of your life.

The Essential Guide for First-Time Homeowners

Maximize Your Investment & Enjoy Your New Home

by Ilona Bray & Alayna Schroeder • $19.99

This reassuring resource is filled with crucial financial advice, real solutions and easy-to-implement ideas that can save you thousands of dollars.

Easy Ways to Lower Your Taxes

Simple Strategies Every Taxpayer Should Know

by Sandra Block & Stephen Fishman • $19.99

Provides useful insights and tactics to help lower your taxes. Learn how to boost tax-free income, get a lower tax rate, defer paying taxes, make the most of deductions—and more!

First-Time Landlord

Your Guide to Renting Out a Single-Family Home

by Attorney Janet Portman, Marcia Stewart & Michael Molinski • $19.99

From choosing tenants to handling repairs to avoiding legal trouble, this book provides the information new landlords need to make a profit and follow the law.

Stopping Identity Theft

10 Easy Steps to Security

by Scott Mitic, CEO, TrustedID, Inc. • $19.99

Don't let an emptied bank account be your first warning sign. This book offers ten strategies to help prevent the theft of personal information.

NOLO *Online Legal Forms*

Nolo offers a large library of legal solutions and forms, created by Nolo's in-house legal staff. These reliable documents can be prepared in minutes.

Online Legal Solutions

- **Incorporation.** Incorporate your business in any state.
- **LLC Formations.** Gain asset protection and pass-through tax status in any state.
- **Wills.** Nolo has helped people make over 2 million wills. Is it time to make or revise yours?
- **Living Trust (avoid probate).** Plan now to save your family the cost, delays, and hassle of probate.
- **Trademark.** Protect the name of your business or product.
- **Provisional Patent.** Preserve your rights under patent law and claim "patent pending" status.

Online Legal Forms

Nolo.com has hundreds of top quality legal forms available for download—bills of sale, promissory notes, nondisclosure agreements, LLC operating agreements, corporate minutes, commercial lease and sublease, motor vehicle bill of sale, consignment agreements and many, many more.

Review Your Documents

Many lawyers in Nolo's consumer-friendly lawyer directory will review Nolo documents for a very reasonable fee. Check their detailed profiles at **lawyers.nolo.com**.